D1316913

June Gould, Ph.D., is the founder and former director of Fairfield University's Summer Writing Process Institute. She acts as a writing consultant to more than twenty-five school districts and for the International Women's Writing Guild, and is currently the director of the Fairchester Institute for Writing, Teaching and Learning. She lives in Westport, Connecticut.

If you are interested in writing workshops led by
June Gould, call 203-226-3279.

The Writer in All of Us

Improving Your Writing Through Childhood Memories

June Gould

Contents

Acknowledgments

Philip Wheelwright, author of *The Burning Fountain*, has said, "A wise [woman] claims nothing for [her] own not even her dreams." This is true for me, for I have come to realize that my personal and professional knowledge takes shape during conversations with others. My thoughts are nurtured and focused when I am part of an interpretive community—whether it is made up of family, friends, or colleagues.

Besides the various friends, acquaintances, and relatives who shaped me, I had very special parents, Ethel and Lou. I am grateful for the decent lives they led, which later gave rise to my interest in the past. My father showed me how to love reading; I cannot remember ever seeing him without a newspaper or a book in his hands. He also introduced me to the fun, beauty, and importance of the larger world beyond our apartment: Prospect Park Lake, the Ocean Parkway bicycle path to Coney Island,

and the cherry trees and rose arbor in the Brooklyn Botanic Garden.

My mother showed me how creativity works. She made beautiful things: my gray chinchilla coat lined with plaid, my white wool jersey hood with red hearts appliquéd at the nape, my multitiered sweet-sixteen cake with the pale pink buttercream rosettes. Her creative pleasure and perseverance were as important for developing my own creativity as all my theoretical readings on the creative process. Without her hands-on examples, I would not have tried my own hand at making poems, stories, or this book.

Many of my present values and ideas come from the educational visions that Joanna Nicholson, Bena Kallick, and I shared with one another and with the thousands of teachers who came to the Teacher's Center at Fairfield, Connecticut, to learn and to teach.

I am also grateful to playwright, director, and artist Shirley Kaplan. In her brilliant collaborative workshops, she helped me find and hold on to my creative direction.

Special thanks need to be given to another community that sharpened and focused my thinking: my doctoral committee. These scholars saw me through the research that informs this book. I am grateful to the late Barbara Myerhoff, author of *Number Our Days,* who believed in my inner resources as a writer and teacher and who encouraged me to research my teaching practice; Mary T. Sheerin, my committee core and now my dear friend, who set the example, never wavering, of a teacher who learns alongside her students; Barbara Kinoy, psychoanalyst, poet, and writer in her field, who helped me see the writing process through a psychoanalytic frame; D. H. Melhem, poet, teacher, and editor, who gave unstintingly of her time and energy and was always supportive of my ideas; Daniel Cheifetz, author of *Theater in My Head,* who stayed actively and critically engaged with my work and whose unflagging interest helped my work grow in depth and precision; and finally, Harry Dunne and Carol Barrett, who contributed their thoughtful and provocative comments.

I am indebted to Hannelore Hahn, the visionary founder and director of the International Women's Writing Guild, for creating an exceptional space that repeatedly inspires my best teaching and writing. She gave me the opportunity to work with extraordinary professional and aspiring writers, many of whom contributed their memory writing to this book.

Fairfield University students, family, colleagues, and friends also contributed their memory writing to *The Writer in All of Us,* and I will always be grateful for their enthusiasm, generosity, and creativity.

For the last several years I have been a member of three remarkable interpretive communities. One is focused on inter-disciplinary studies, another on feminist novels, and the third on the members' own writing. I am grateful to the participants in each of these groups for their stimulating and compassionate interpretation of texts that have found their way directly and indirectly into this book and my life.

My work as a writer, researcher, and teacher has been in-fluenced by the ground-breaking research and writings of Ann E. Berthoff, James Britton, Lucy Calkins, Peter Elbow, Janet Emig, Toby Fulwiler, Dixie Goswami, Donald Graves, James Grey, Elaine Maimon, James Moffett, Donald Murray, and Son-dra Perl. I am grateful to have benefited from their insights and contributions to the field of writing; they have provided me with the framework with which to construct this book.

Special fanfare also has to go to the interdisciplinary think-ers: Betsy Brinson, Joan Carey, Helene Fagin, Posy Gering, Leslie Mills, Jeffrey Rubin, Mary T. Sheerin, Kenneth Tewel, Denis Walsh, and Kathleen Williams. They have contributed to this book by providing me with insights from their feminist, psy-choanalytic, literary, philosophical, musical, medical, theatrical, and educational perspectives. They have not only stretched my thinking, they have also captured my affection.

A bouquet of roses and unending gratitude go to my agent, Frances Goldin, who stood by me every step of the way before, during, and after writing this book. She is special—a woman of integrity, perseverance, and beauty.

In addition, I owe a debt of gratitude to author and editor Jerry Gross for recognizing this book's worth.

Last but not least, I dedicate this book with love and warmest appreciation to my husband, Larry; to our daughters, Laura and Elizabeth; and to our son, Gerry. All allowed me to close the door of my office while they led their own lives. I could not have spent time writing and remembering unless I knew that when I left my computer they would be there—alive, warm, and wonderful.

The Writer in All of Us

Introduction

Most of the basic material a writer works with is acquired before the age of fifteen.
—WILLA CATHER

This book is focused on you. It is designed to help you realize your potential both as a writer and as a person. I believe that we have potential for growth and change in all areas of our lives. Despite all our problems—financial worries, family jealousies, anxieties over the future, sadness about a failed relationship, fears of illness and death—we also have a passion to shape personally meaningful lives, to understand ourselves and the world around us, and to grow and branch out in positive directions. Despite all of our personal and interpersonal concerns, something within us, perhaps our childhood wonder, still trusts that others can be transformed, too. We try to stay open to new experiences, people, and ideas; we have an emotional connection to our memories; and deep down we feel we are just a larger version of our childhood selves.

My childhood memories now play an important part in my life as a teacher and a writer. But this was not always so. How did I discover their importance? For sixteen years I grew as a college writing teacher, an administrator of a teacher's center, a poet, a wife and a mother. But suddenly I found myself stagnating in both my professional and my personal life. It became increasingly hard for me to create new programs, new solutions to family problems, new writing workshops, poems, stories, and articles. I felt out of touch with my internal resources for new ideas and life direction. I had been nurturing and facilitating other people's creativity, but I had been neglecting my own. I yearned for a writing outlet that would call on my creativity and at the same time unleash the inborn writer—and person—caged within me.

I remembered twenty years ago, when I had let my Bedford-Stuyvesant students choose the topics they wanted to write about. They had written about love and beatings, birth and foster families, hunger and fulfillment—and their writing had improved. They seemed to have been born with the ability to express themselves well in writing. Now I wrote like them, about how I had caught a whiskered catfish in a Prospect Park pond, and I reexperienced the combination of delight and revulsion that I had felt as the fish squirmed in my hands. With this, the mechanics of writing sprang to me naturally. I did not need explicit formulas and abstract exercises on how to "write a good lead line," on how to "show not tell," or on how to "find my own voice." Writing researcher Ken Macrorie explains how this worked: As I wrote, the smells and sounds of the past affected my body, and I began to shape my writing with the rhythms and images that belonged to those events and with words that sounded out my feelings.

Amazed, I was delighted to see that in the process of writing about my memories and in my constant examinations and reexaminations of the meaning of the events of my life, I had released the powers of my mind with which I could imagine the possibility of changing my own reality. In this process I discovered that I had reclaimed my self as well as my natural writing self.

Over the years, I have taught writing to a still growing audience of approximately ten thousand students, including writ-

ing teachers; writers; elementary, high school, and college students; helping professionals; businesspeople; and the general
public.

I help my students imagine the possibility of changing their
realities by showing them how to project their childhood images
into words on paper, sort through their images of the past with
their pens, carry them in their journals and their briefcases so
that they can *refine, revise,* and *reshape* their view of themselves,
their writing, and their world. I give them a brief survey of what
memories and memory writing have meant to writers both in the
past and in the present.

For example, the ancient Greeks called upon their goddess
Memory (Mnemosyne, daughter of Earth and Sky, mother of the
Muses) to inspire their speeches and writing. Sam Keen encouraged mythmaking and autobiographical storytelling in his
To a Dancing God. He believes that "in the depth of each man's
biography lies the story of all men." Marcel Proust used his
memories in *Remembrance of Things Past* as a map for discovering
his identity and thereby took his place in the world of literature.

T. S. Eliot meditated on the past in *Four Quartets,* in order
to shed light on the present, while James McConkey used memory as a map, in *Court of Memory,* to find his way to the spiritual
world. Maxine Greene wrote in *Language Arts,* a magazine for
teachers, "If we ourselves can reach back to that original pres-
entness [in childhood], we may recapture something of where
cognition begins."

The reasons for writing about one's memories are numerous
and varied. Each person evokes his or her memories for a different
purpose. Nathalie Sarraute said in *Childhood,* "We grope our way
along, forever searching . . . we push it . . . so long as it eventually finds some fertile ground where it can develop, where it
can perhaps manage to live."

When I work with my students, I know that, whatever their
reasons for wanting to explore their pasts, teaching them to write
begins with my recognition that each comes to the workshop
with different memories and feelings. My job is to be open to

them and to help them be open to themselves. "What images, feelings, or concerns from your childhood are here with you today?" I ask, whether the students have never written before or are professional writers.

I stroll hand in hand with my students, and I try to focus on them and on their wonder rather than on the abstract subject of learning to write. I can tap into their human instincts to write if I help them realize that their lives and memories are worth telling stories about, and if I help zoom in on topics of fundamental importance to *them.*

The content of my workshops is not abstract formulas or quick-fix gimmicks but rather the fiber and texture, the laughter and sorrow of real life. Because we are free from complicated assignments and rules, we can respond to gifts and surprises, to the many discoveries, *to memories* as they wiggle and squirm like my catfish and nudge their whiskered noses into our present lives.

In his acceptance speech for the Oscar at the 1986 Academy Awards ceremony, Steven Spielberg stated that the creativity for his movies comes from his childhood in Arizona. He, like the writers I have just quoted, harnesses the power of his memories to fuel his creativity, self-development, and writing growth.

Do not be afraid of your own growing power. Listen to what M. C. Richards said in *The Crossing Point:* "The child in [us] is [our] growing tip, alive throughout our lifespan. One of the labors of adulthood is to befriend in ourselves those handicapped and underdeveloped parts of our nature which we have set aside." When you awaken your most distant memories, you will be able to retrieve and nurture the slumbering and frightened writer inside of you. As you awaken your childhood memories, remember that thousands have made this journey before you, and thousands will make it after you. Rub the sleep out of your eyes, and get ready to join the multitudes who know that remembering is worth it, not only for the way you live now but for the way you will live in the future.

The chapters that follow present tested childhood-memory writing exercises from my workshops. They will take you through the processes for unleashing the natural, creative, inborn writer caged within *all* of us. They are based on current writing research; on my experiences as a writer, as a writing workshop leader, and as a writing consultant; and on the words and wisdom of well-known writers, educators, philosophers, and psychologists.

Before I move on, I should like to invoke the Greek goddess Memory through this prayer-poem read by Lorraine Ackerman at the International Women's Writing Guild Conference in 1983. Perhaps you would like to say it aloud before we begin our journey together.

> May Mnemosyne, Daughter of Earth and Sky,
> Wife of Zeus, Mother of the Muses
> Bless us abundantly with her spirit.
> May her daughters, the Muses,
> Bless us with their spirits.
>
> May we, her [children] too,
> Journey from forgetfulness to remembrance,
> So we may discover once again what we already know.
> For in memory we see it All.
>
> Let the solitude sound its voice within us,
> And bring forth the new story
> And may we become the means
> For another's transformation.

Unleashing the Writer in All of Us

1

Among the invisible tools of creative individuals is their ability to hold on to the specific texture of their past. Their skill is akin to that of a rural family who lives through the winter on food stored in their root cellar.

—VERA JOHN-STEINER

A student at my Summer Writing Institute at Fairfield University in Connecticut wrote an imaginary letter to herself from her dead great-grandmother. She cried when she read it to our class, and so did the rest of us. She later asked me when we were going to do exercises on the components of good writing. I told her the components were already there in her letter: an authentic voice, sensory detail, focus, emotion, and appropriate choice of genre.

"But I did that by accident," she said. "How am I going to do it again when I have to write a story or a report for another class?" It was very important for her to be able to separate skills for good writing from her emotions and interests. Writing had to be serious, about someone or something else. She felt that her own feelings and experiences were somehow frivolous and sentimental.

We have learned to value other people's writing rules and exercises over our own. Where did we learn this? Unfortunately, from our schools and teachers! Remember the way you were taught to write? Let me remind you.

THE OLD WRITING CLASSROOM

I don't want you looking out at the trees turning color in the street, wasting your time peeking at the window washer hanging by a strap outside our windows, or staring at the women picking up their bread and cupcakes from the Dugan delivery man. Because you have writing "work" to do!
—MISS HATTON, P.S. 92, Brooklyn, 1947

I was ten years old, in the fourth row of Miss Hatton's large, high-ceilinged classroom. Its walls were painted institutional green, a color that was supposed to be good for our eyes. Forty-five of us were sitting in bolted-down desks and chairs. Our eyes riveted to the front of the room, our hands clasped.

Above the blackboard was an alphabet. Fire drill and air-raid instructions were posted next to the door. Our corrected spelling tests were displayed on the bulletin board at the back of the room, but no compositions were displayed there, "because," Miss Hatton said, our papers "had so many mistakes and they looked ugly."

Miss Hatton was assigning our composition topic. "Write about what it means to be a good American. I will allow only one draft, and you must write it perfectly on white-lined composition paper. You will be penalized if you erase. Think carefully before you write."

I always made mistakes, and after I turned my composition in, Miss Hatton bled red ink all over my paper. Since we were never given time to rewrite, I soon lost faith in myself as a writer. Because I had to struggle so much, I concluded that I just was not "born to write."

In truth, the ability to shape experience artistically was a gift I possessed from early childhood, but I was so dissatisfied with the results of my writing in my youth that I did not believe it. My "nonwriter" feeling began in school with Miss Hatton, who made me feel stupid, and the feeling lasted for years. Every time I wrote, even in adulthood, I envisioned Miss Hatton sitting on my shoulder pointing her nasty, bleeding pen at my mistakes.

But worrying about correctness was only part of my writing problem. Miss Hatton had never shown me *how to write,* and so I was left with my own idiosyncratic way of composing. I still blush when I remember my tactics.

I would procrastinate until the last minute; then I would finally go to the library with my notebook and ballpoint pen and sit and stare at a blank page. I would doodle for a while as I watched other people copying out of books or thumbing through magazines, and I would feel completely defeated by the emptiness in front of me. I would return to my home with very little written—maybe a paragraph or two copied from a book. I always started with someone else's words because I was afraid of the mistakes I would make with my own.

After dinner I would go into my room and slam the door behind me. Flicking the top of my ballpoint pen nervously, I would glower at the paper, waiting for inspiration. Discouraged, I would get some soda from the kitchen, look around for a snack, and take the Ring Dings back to my room, only to become distracted again. Noticing that my *Seventeen* magazines were out of order, I would organize them, or I would phone my friend Rochelle with the latest gossip.

While my parents slept and our apartment was quiet, I would put some confused words down on paper. My writing always made me feel as if I were lost in the middle of a dense forest. I had trouble finding entrances into my ideas, and even more trouble finding my way out. One thought led to another, but nothing ever seemed to make sense. Reading my writing back to myself made me feel scatterbrained and incoherent. It reminded me of the way I felt when I was learning to ride a bike for the first time: totally out of control, incompetent, and scared. But it is one thing to feel jerky and scared on a bike and finally with practice to be able to ride it smoothly and gracefully; it is another to continue to write like a beginner. I saw myself reflected in the fragmented, sloppy, mazelike words on my page, and I hated myself. My writing mirrored me, and it was disorienting and frightening.

I hated the assigned compositions because they were always so far from the papers I meant to write, and they were nothing like the professional writing my teachers gave me to read. But I had no idea how to improve, and so I avoided the entire process whenever possible. I stopped writing for pleasure and gratification.

Since the nineteenth century, many of our writing classes have been conducted by teachers like Miss Hatton. They have told us, and some are still telling us, that we will never learn to write because we do not pay attention to the corrections they make on our papers or to the prescriptions in our grammar books. They have saddled us with writing rules that were intended to constrain our mistakes, but those constraints keep us from developing a repertoire of writing strategies and a sustained relationship with language. Remember the rules? Remember how we felt about them?

- *Pay attention to the corrections on your paper, and don't make those mistakes again on another assignment.*

But how could I learn to revise and correct my mistakes when I was not given time to rewrite the paper that contained all the errors?

- *Write about what I assign to you.*

The assigned topics were so boring. They couldn't compete with what I had on my mind: dating, a grandfather's heart attack, my mother's hospitalization, a lost ring, a party.

- *Write a poem, essay, report, or story.*

They never told me how. When they did, it was a formula to follow, not a handle on a topic that would lead me to authentic, deeply felt, and meaningful work.

- *Write the composition for me and for my eyes only.*

I was so afraid of my teachers' criticisms that I restricted myself and wrote papers that were dull and lifeless.

- *No talking or looking at anyone else's work during writing time.*

I was dying to see what other kids were writing. I needed ideas, models—*anything* to help me write.

• *Think before you write.*

I couldn't think before I wrote—I kept losing my ideas. I felt dumb because I thought the really smart kids could do what my writing teachers asked. I did my thinking while I was writing or after I wrote, rarely before, and I felt ashamed of that process and saw it as a flaw.

• *Write objectively. Keep yourself out of your writing.*

When I kept myself out of my writing, I felt like a robot. My words sounded mechanical and hollow.

• *Learn to write by memorizing and following rules. If you learn to diagram and punctuate a sentence, outline your composition, and recognize all the modes of writing, such as poetry, the essay, the report, and so on, your writing will improve.*

I could rattle off these rules in the abstract, but I could not apply them to my actual writing. In fact, the more rules I memorized, the more inhibited I became. I was afraid of breaking the rules and getting a bad grade.

• *Write once a month, once or twice a semester, or once a week.*

I always needed more time to sort out the complicated maze of ideas I had generated in my papers. But because I never had time in class, my choices were either to oversimplify my writing or to allow it to remain confused. Of course, neither option satisfied me or my teachers.

PROCESS WRITING

> You need only claim the events of your life to make yourself yours. When you truly possess all you have been and done, which may take some time, you are fierce with reality.
>
> —FLORIDA SCOTT-MAXWELL

Unfortunately, because our teachers were trained to look only at our mistakes, they believed that knowledge of indirect objects, iambic pentameter, outlining before writing, thesis statements, and written forms would help us write. But writers do not begin a piece by saying, "I want to write a short story to fulfill my logical outline of the story." They write, like Émile Zola, "to live out loud," or like E. M. Forster, "to know what I think," or like Sherwood Anderson, who thought "the whole glory of writing lies in the fact that it forces us out of ourselves and into the lives of others."

Writing genres are not carved in stone. A real writer may begin with a conversation or a letter to a colleague and end up with several lines for a poem or essay. Dialogue and description can be found not only in plays and novels but also in journal entries and poems, persuasive essay writing often emerges from narratives, and so on.

In spite—or because—of our writing teachers' efforts, most of us could not or would not write under their supervision. But happily, a revolution has been going on recently in the field of teaching writing. For the last fifteen years, researchers who formerly looked at how a poem, story, novel, essay, or play was constructed are now focusing on what *processes* writers use. They are asking, What kinds of topics do writers naturally choose? How do memories feed our imaginations and our writing? What do people do when they write, and how do writers and their writing change over time? Researchers want to know if there is a difference between the way skilled and unskilled writers work. They have helped writing teachers concentrate on their students' writing processes rather than on correcting finished products. They have come up with six fascinating observations that have profoundly affected thousands of writing teachers in all English-speaking countries of the world. Their findings have helped us shift our teaching style to helping students write from within rather than from rules imposed from without. In fact, all my courses and this book are designed around the following current research findings, which have begun to revolutionize the teaching of writing:

- Most of us go through five interactive and recursive stages when we write: we *rehearse*, we *prewrite*, we *draft*, we *revise*, and we *edit*. Becoming aware of our writing process enables us to use each of its stages until our writing develops into what we envision it could be.

- We can be coached to write well during each of these five stages of the writing process.
- When we shift our concentration from mistakes on the paper to ourselves and our experiences, our writing improves.
- Writing also improves at the point of choosing the topic we are drawn to, and that magnetic topic is generated by our memories, feelings, and concerns.
- Feedback from colleagues, friends, family, or teachers during each stage of the writing process helps clarify our intentions and motivates revision.
- Writing is not an act of product analysis but is first and foremost an act of definition—of what we remember, what we know, and what we feel, see, touch, and taste, all of which constitute the many sides of who we are.

These findings describe what produces effective writing. The process is not a fragmented, rigid, analytic breakdown of the mechanics of writing; rather, it develops our ability to move flexibly and often recursively through a series of stages. For the process to work, however, *you* must be central, and your stories, memories, feelings, and concerns must be like a song, sounding and ringing in your thoughts and on your paper.

The Process-Writing Classroom

Children write about what is alive and vital and real for them—and their writing becomes the curriculum.

—LUCY CALKINS

Many writing classrooms, from kindergarten through graduate school, have changed dramatically since this recent research has been disseminated to teachers. I have consulted in elementary schools, high schools, and colleges to help teachers across the disciplines shift from one-draft, teacher-directed, lecture-type classrooms to multidraft, student-initiated, workshop environments.

This process is a far cry from Miss Hatton's rigid writing dicta, and from well-meant but stifling writing assignments such as "I Am a Winter Leaf Falling Off a Tree," "My Life as a Drop of Water," or "If I Ran the School." Process-writing classrooms leave creativity in the hands of the students. The classrooms are student centered, predictable, and secure; since writing is unpredictable and risky, students seem to flourish best in safe and simple environments. The courses are designed by teachers who want to help their students become fluent, independent writers, so process-writing teachers give their students both time and security.

Here is how eighth-grader Kristine Schiebel of Westport, Connecticut, describes her process-writing classroom:

> My 8th grade English room is special because it has poetry covering the walls and hanging from the ceiling. I feel dignified in here seeing that my writing is "published."
>
> As you approach the room the arrangement of the desks in a semi circle tells you that everyone learns as a group and shares their thoughts here. We are positioned to see the expressions and feelings on each person's face. This special arrangement forms the "Writer's Workshop."
>
> During the workshop we write about ourselves, our memories. We can make many drafts before we hand our revision in to our teacher. Sometimes before I write a draft I "freewrite," or "map" my ideas. I always have a chance to get feedback from other kids in the class. Everyone, including my teacher, helps me revise and edit.
>
> We help each other by listening and responding to each person's writing in small groups or in the whole class. My teacher, Miss Ernst, also confers with us individually and helps us as we go along, but we are the center and the life of the room.

Do not feel cheated after reading this! You have not irre-
vocably missed out on a wonderfully productive and creative
writing experience. This book, in fact, is designed like the
process-writing classroom. The format, which is predictable and
supportive, will enable you to focus on yourself and on your
memories rather than on complicated techniques. It will give
you a second chance to learn how to write by taking you on a
writing journey to awaken and restore the writer in you that got
squelched or flattened or shoved aside by your old-fashioned
writing teachers.

Thousands of my students and I myself have gone through
this writing reeducation, and we can tell you that as you get in
touch with your memories and writing process and restore them
to full working order, you will get tremendous pleasure. For those
of you who have already learned to write in a process-writing
classroom, this book will be an added boon because it will maintain your writing excitement and at the same time boost you
toward ever greater writing capability.

Coaching Instead of Criticizing

Capitalization, spelling, punctuation—these are touted as the basics in
writing when they represent . . . merely the conventions, the amenities
for recording the outcome of the process.

—JANET EMIG

When I learned to ride a bicycle, my father held the back of the
seat and ran alongside, holding me in balance. He kept talking,
coaching me as I wobbled along: "Look directly in front of you,
keep pedaling, don't stop. Come on, keep a steady pace. Good,
that's right, sit up straight, light touch on the handlebars. No,
don't look behind you, don't stop, you're doing fine." He didn't
lecture me and test me on bicycle parts before he let me get on
the bike for the first time, nor did he make me stop and start
again every time I looked behind me or wiggled the handlebars
in the wrong direction. *He encouraged me to keep going; he critiqued*

my riding and gave me advice only after I had gone some distance and he had seen my progress.

It takes a long time to learn to do something new, to incorporate strange rules and make the rules work each time we need them. I improved as a bike rider only after my father gave me plenty of time to practice the skill and after he gave me suggestions as I went along based on my progress. "You were leaning over toward the right when you rode just now," he'd say. "Try pushing your handlebars to the left next time. You don't have to pump so hard—you can glide sometimes, too."

Being coached gives me confidence, helps me correct difficulties as they are happening, pushes me toward self-assured mastery. Red corrections get me so uptight and confused that I produce the very mistakes that the rules are meant to prevent: confused syntax, fractured grammar, and constrained fluency. I'm not saying that we should not learn the rules of standard English, but we will have a much better chance of mastering those rules over the long term if we are coached in the context of our actual writing. In this book, I will help you watch how you write about your childhood memories, and I will coach your writing as you go along.

TEN WAYS WRITING ABOUT CHILDHOOD MEMORIES UNLEASHES YOUR INNER WRITER

1. *Childhood memories allow us to reclaim our childhood voice, which is the fire that fuels our authentic adult voice.* As children, we had no difficulty expressing how we felt, but school and other societal influences forced our voices underground. Expressing our memories unearths that voice.

2. *Childhood memories build the foundation for creative and imaginative writing.* Memories and our power to imagine are intertwined. When we remember, our image-making powers are released, and our writing becomes creative, imaginative, and delightful.

3. *Childhood memories stimulate sequential, connected, flowing,*

comprehensive, and complete writing. Many of our memories are rituals: our bedtime routine, our route to school, the unfolding of a wedding or funeral, the way we were treated when we were sick. Because rituals are remembered complete, our memory writing is comprehensive and "whole."

4. *Childhood memories generate emotion.* They are a natural source of deeply felt and keenly experienced events. When we write about them, our writing is infused with how we felt in the past and how we are feeling as we write about the past.

5. *Childhood memories motivate revision.* All writers want their writing to sound close to the image they have in mind, but childhood-memory writers have a further stake in getting their words right: their memories represent them, and they want that representation to be accurate.

6. *Childhood memories contain meaning.* They give us a context in which we can interpret ourselves and the world around us.

7. *Childhood memories stimulate readers' imaginations.* When we recall childhood events, we actually "see" the scenes. As we describe those scenes in writing, they become alive in the minds and imaginations of readers.

8. *Childhood memories excavate what we already know about ourselves but do not know we know.* Our brains have recorded, through our senses, much more than we are aware of at any moment. The material for writing is inside us, but it needs to be recovered, relived, understood, and shared.

9. *Childhood memories provide models for writing well in every field.* Once our latent writing knowledge is brought to our consciousness, that knowledge can be used in other writing fields such as business writing, school papers, personal correspondence, fiction, political writing, screenwriting, and so on.

10. *Childhood memories generate complex and interesting writing.* Because childhood is elusive, intricate, and paradoxical, we use higher-order thinking skills—questioning, evaluating,

analyzing, and synthesizing—to understand it. Trying to understand the complexity of our memories pushes us to make leaps in our thinking, which lead to leaps in our writing.

HOW TO USE THIS BOOK

Writing is a struggle against silence.

—CARLOS FUENTES

The exercises throughout this book are intended to help you develop your inner voice by *prewriting, drafting,* and *revising* brief childhood memories. I will then help you shape these memories into personal narratives, family stories, portraits, letters, dialogues, and poems. The pieces will be like photographs that you can look back on, muse over, and ponder at your leisure.

In Chapter 2 you will find out *where, when,* and *how* to begin writing. Through the meditation exercises in Chapter 3, I will help you retrieve your memories. Chapters 4 and 5 will take you through the *prewriting* and *drafting* stages of your writing process, during which you will surprise and delight yourself with memories you did not know you had. Through each memory-writing experience, you will find yourself developing a receptivity to childhood memories and childhood language, with all its details, tone, rhythm, forms, repetitions, and patterns. Then, as you continue to draw on your memories and write about them, you will reclaim the ability to sound like your true self.

Each chapter of exercises will also show you how to keep a Process Journal of your vignettes so that you can evaluate and take charge of your own writing and personal progress. In Chapter 6 I will show you how to develop a writing response group so you can find out, in each stage of the writing process, how your vision affects an audience by hearing their responses to your writing. Chapter 7 will help you take one of your favorite memories through the *revising* and *editing* stages.

In chapters 8 through 10, you will be able to carry over your newfound writing skills so that writing about childhood memories can enhance all spheres of your academic, professional, and personal life.

At the end of this book is a bibliography of writing-related books, articles, and periodicals.

2

Getting Ready to Write

*Pursue, keep up with, circle round and round
your life, as a dog does his master's chaise. Do
what you love. Know your own bone, gnaw at
it, bring it, unearth it, and gnaw it still.*
— HENRY DAVID THOREAU

NOTEBOOKS

Get yourself several spiral-bound stenographers' notebooks for
the exercises in this book. Stenographers' notebooks have a line
down the middle of each page, which is perfect for our purposes.
Your writing for the memory exercises—original thoughts and
lists (these are not restricted to memories)—will go to the left
of the ruled line. Writings for your Process Journal—revisions,
reflections, further ideas, and questions—will go to the right.
The Memories column is where you will write about your childhood. Your Process Journal, which runs alongside your recollections, will enable you to converse with, reflect on, and analyze
both your memories and the attributes of your own writing process.

If you were to scan my own notebooks, here are the kinds of things you would see on one side of the center line or the other:

- lists of memories
- descriptions of places and people in my childhood
- conversations from my childhood
- reflections on my writing process
- letters to myself from my ancestors
- family stories
- notes I have taken from TV programs, newspapers, books, magazines, speeches
- freewriting
- mapping to show how a piece might be organized
- drafts
- quotations from writers, artists, musicians, scientists, any creative people
- art postcards from museums
- blue, yellow, or rainbow-hued pages
- photographs from my childhood
- newspaper clippings
- titles of books I want to read or have read
- imaginary letters to or from my family or childhood friends
- writing schedules that help me with deadlines

I go nowhere without my notebook. I write in my car while waiting to pick up my children from ballet or baseball, while I wait for my dentist, on airplanes, in my hammock, in bed at night, and while waiting to meet someone for lunch. A stenographer's notebook fits into my briefcase, pocketbook, or canvas boat bag and is convenient to have with me wherever I am, no matter what I am doing.

Just having your notebook close at hand will stimulate the flow of your memories and your creativity. It will help you make use of the "in-between" times, which for many of us are the only times available for writing. I write for at least fifteen minutes at one sitting, but I also try to squeeze five minutes in, here or there, throughout the day. You will find that if you write every day, you will fill a notebook in about a month.

I often go back through my notebooks to get ideas for current writing projects and to see how my thinking or feelings have or have not changed. Because you are not following rules, looking back at your writing process will help you to get in touch with what *you* do when you write. Then, once you are aware of your own process, you can repeat what has worked for you and discard what is dysfunctional.

Get your critical writing teacher off your shoulder. If you view the notebook as a place where you can be utterly yourself, you will not feel foolish when you make the mistakes essential in discovering what it is you really want to say. It will help your writing if you can share your notebook with others, but since the notebook is really a physical manifestation of your thoughts, memories, and imagination, you have every right to decide which parts you want others to respond to and which parts you want to keep private.

WRITING TOOLS

I like to think about the tone of my writing. I ask myself, What color does my writing evoke in my mind's eye? If I have time, I even softly tint the page that contains a memory with crayon: a sad memory gets pale blue, a happy one is bright yellow, an angry image is red or black. If you take the time to give color to your memories, you will become more conscious of the feeling, mood, tone, and attitude embedded in your writing. The more you are conscious of what you are doing, the more you can control and shape your writing into the images you have in your mind.

Lots of my students like to use pens to color-code their feelings, moods, or memories. At the outset, you may want to get two pens, one for the left-hand column in your notebook and another for the right. That way you will rapidly perceive differences among your lists, drafts, revisions, and process reflections. You may want to use thick Magic Markers, pencils,

pens, or a computer. Whatever you choose, repeat your choice
if it works for you, or revise or delete it if it does not.

FINDING YOUR NICHE

You need to find a place where you can write steadily for fifteen
minutes. I write in bed at night before going to sleep. While I
am relaxed, in the state between wakefulness and sleep, my
memories, images, and feelings seem to flow effortlessly out of
my pen. I keep my notebook on the night table next to my bed
while I sleep. I often jot down memories or images from dreams
in the middle of the night. When I refer back to my nocturnal
scribblings, they seem to take me to a deeper place in my memory,
to a place harder to reach when I am in my "mother," "teacher,"
or "researcher" role.

I hope you will recognize the importance of capturing every
stray memory. Ralph Waldo Emerson once said, "If you do not
write those memories down when they occur, you may lose them
by morning, and . . . you shall never find that perception again;
never . . . but perhaps years, ages, and I know not what events
and worlds may lie between you and its return!"

Wherever you decide to write, pay attention to what happens to your memories and your writing style when you compose
there. Different rooms influence my memories and my writing.
My kitchen, for example, stimulates childhood images of meal-
times with my family: my mother's pot roast and brownies, the
view of a city courtyard out of our kitchen window, my father
rolling a cigarette and smoking it in a holder while drinking his
coffee and reading World War II headlines in *The New York
Times*. When I write in the kitchen, I want to write kitchen
poems, or dialogues with the people who used to live in the
apartments outside our window.

Writing outdoors when the weather is warm gives me spring
fever. I can visualize photographs taken of me in 1948 during
Prospect Park strolls, taste the Cracker Jacks, feel my new navy-

blue double-breasted coat with the pearl-gray buttons. I feel expansive and ready to write the great American novel about growing up in Brooklyn!

FINDING THE TIME

I don't know whether the inward work is achieving something or whether it is simply the autumn light, but I begin to see my way again, which means to resume *myself*.

—MAY SARTON

If you are a busy young parent, try writing while your baby naps. Perhaps you can carry your notebook in a knapsack with your baby's bottles and diapers. Actually, writing about your memories may be a boon to your baby; it may help you identify more completely with his or her feelings and needs.

If you have older children, many of the things they do and say will trigger memories of your own childhood. They will help you recall what you did when you were young. Keep your notebook with you while you spend time with your kids in your home, on vacation, and while watching them explore, play, and learn to speak.

If you are a businessperson, perhaps you can put your travel time to productive use by writing on airplanes. Or how about during coffee breaks, on your commuter train, or while waiting for a client, a tennis court, or a haircut? If weekends are best for you, try to set aside hefty chunks of time so that you can write an idea through to completion. Of course, vacations give you the ultimate freedom to move away from the demands of your work and toward relaxing, remembering, and writing.

Many teachers—as well as principals—write in their classrooms during the time their students are writing. Not only does this give them an opportunity to write but it also lets students know that they take writing seriously. My research with teachers and principals shows that their own memories are triggered by observing children in their schools and that remembering their childhoods also helps them empathize with their students—essential to good teaching.

Those of you who are members of the helping professions—such as nurses, psychologists, doctors, lawyers, and counselors—often have a pressing need to establish and maintain an authentic, strong identity to meet the emotional and time-consuming needs of your clients. Some of you may have time to write between appointments with clients, but others may have to use weekends or vacations for larger chunks of time. Writing about your childhood will enhance your understanding and expertise; at the same time, it will help you keep your professional self rooted in your authentic self.

If you are a student, why not write during study halls or between classes? Winter and spring breaks are nice blocks of time to spend with your memories and your notebook. If you write about childhood memories before you write an assignment, your writing muscles will be warmed up, and your assignment writing will flow and be infused with your authentic voice.

Making the decision to start remembering will lower a long fishing line into the depths of your past. Once you have decided to write, you will be surprised at how many memories start tugging at you. The whole world—nature, family, books, TV, news, movies, conversation—will seem to exist solely to remind you of your childhood. Chapter 3 will help you haul in the line with your memories and show you how to preserve them in your notebooks.

Rehearsal: Hauling in the Line

3

*Writing is hauling in a long line from the depths
to find out what things are strung on it.*
—JAMES MOFFETT

Writing does not happen without preparation. Like an athlete warming up her muscles before an event, I stretch my writing muscles before I write, to focus my mental energy. *Rehearsing* is the way I do it. Rehearsing helps me get started; it enables me to generate topics as well as ideas about those topics. It kindles my imagination and builds momentum for the writing that will follow. And it focuses my thinking so that I will have fewer revisions to make later on.

It is often difficult for me, I admit, to put off the actual act of writing, to let myself talk, think, read, and dream about the topic that I will finally write about. I have so many things to juggle in my life: family, friends, colleagues, my teaching and writing careers. Like you, I want to tie up loose ends and get everything done so I can go on to the next meeting, deadline, workshop, or assignment.

Nevertheless, slowing down to plan what I will say is worth

the effort. Rehearsal is not just a stage to get past; it is an attitude, a way of being in the world. When I am rehearsing, I become supersensitive to everything going on both inside and outside of me. This heightened awareness helps transform me into a writer and my memories into stories.

USING THE WRITING-MEDITATION CONNECTION

Meditation affects your life and your life shapes your meditation. It goes both ways. Less busyness in life brings greater richness in meditation. This richness makes you content with less of the trimmings of outer life. As this process continues, less is more.

—RAM DASS

Meditation is a way of rehearsing that helps me apprehend the world through a writer's eyes. It helps me block out the outside world so that I can attune myself to my own internal rhythms, which are interconnected with the rhythms of the universe. Meditation also loosens my conscious control so that I can be transported toward the deep streams of memory as well as toward what writing researcher James Moffett has called "a confluence of streams . . . which trigger, interrupt, and reinforce each other." Meditation can take us back to these primordial rhythms, where our perception of the world began and from which our creativity springs.

The exercise sections that follow will help you to recollect all the fascinating, vital, impracticable, impressive, foolish, significant, and essential things that touched your life during your childhood by way of four meditations. They will then help you put those memories into thematic written memory lists, called a Memory Inventory, that you can draw on for future use.

There is no "right" way to do the four meditations in this section. You may want to experience all of them in one sitting, or you may find it more helpful to do each one separately on a different day of the week. You may want to repeat the same meditation every day for a week before moving on to the next one. In the process of experiencing these meditations, you may find that you prefer one over the others; make a mental note of your preference so that you can use it when you need it.

You may wish to record the instructions for the meditations on a tape recorder before you begin them. This will help you concentrate as you do the meditations.

Find a quiet place where you will not be interrupted. Relax your body, and allow your awareness to heighten. Allow five minutes for each meditation.

Meditation 1: Getting Rid of Distractions

As long as we are busy running in circles on the surface of the mind we will never penetrate to the depths.

—KATHLEEN MCDONALD

This meditation will show you what you are thinking here and now that might be distracting you from trying to find the stories in your childhood. Do this meditation before doing exercises to develop a Memory Inventory or whenever you need to write but are finding it difficult to let go of the things that distract you.

First choose an object to gaze at. This can be an actual object from your childhood, a photograph, or something natural that you might have seen as a child, such as a flower, a shell, or a leaf.

Once you are in your meditation spot, sit comfortably, feet flat on the ground, hands resting open in your lap. Place your object in front of you, where you can see it easily.
RELAX FIVE SECONDS.

Let your eyes focus softly on your object. Relax your eyes; let them be a camera, receiving only the sight in front of them. RELAX FIVE SECONDS.

Focus on your object and try to see the childhood memories connected to it. Keep track of where your mind takes you. If it takes you back to the present or into the future, note where you seem to be drifting, but try to keep your mind in the past.
DO THIS FOR ABOUT THREE MINUTES.

Now let your mind go wherever it wants to, let it wander. Observe where it goes. Relax and let go.
RELAX TEN SECONDS.

Meditation 2: Tapping into the Stream

To begin with, you must teach the unconscious to flow into the channel of writing. . . . The first step toward being a writer is to hitch your unconscious mind to your writing arm.

—DOROTHEA BRANDE

Use this meditation to tap into your memory stream. You will need it to develop your Memory Inventory. Do this meditation before undertaking the memory exercises in this book or whenever you need to write for personal or professional reasons.

Sit comfortably and take a deep breath. Breathe in through your nose and out through your mouth. Let yourself go as you breathe. Feel the tension go out of your neck, back, arms, and legs. Be as relaxed as you can.
RELAX FIVE SECONDS.

Close your eyes. Focus your thoughts in the center of your forehead.
RELAX FIVE SECONDS.

See your memories as images or pictures rather than as sentences. Every time you *see* a memory, say "Memory, Memory" to yourself and then continue watching. If you see or hear something that is not a memory, label it by saying "No, no," and try to push it away. If something else happens, such as hearing music or seeing colors or shapes, label that, too, by saying "Music," "Color," or "Shape."
RELAX FIVE SECONDS.

See yourself learning something new, such as bike riding, ice skating, swimming, tying shoelaces, making a bed, broad jumping, playing baseball, planting seeds, playing checkers.
CONTINUE FOR THREE OR FOUR MINUTES.

Meditation 3: Finding Your Childhood Voice

> We should be satisfied with whatever does appear, even if it is just a blur
> of color or a minor detail. . . . Thus it is very important to be relaxed
> and free of expectations.
>
> —KATHLEEN MCDONALD

Use this meditation before developing a Memory Inventory, before undertaking the memory exercises, and whenever you write
about your childhood.

Sit comfortably. Breathe deeply in through your nose and
out through your mouth. Let your body and your mind relax.
Leave the hectic world outside you for now. Slowly let your
nervous system settle down.
RELAX FIVE TO TEN SECONDS.

Focus on your breathing as you go inside yourself. Feel the
rising and falling of your breath. As you breathe in, say to yourself
"In, in"; as you breathe out, say "Out, out."
CONTINUE FOR THREE TO FOUR MINUTES.

Send your mind back to your childhood. See yourself in
school. Feel the child inside you breathing in and out. What
were you doing? What were you feeling? Who was there with
you? Listen for your child-voice speaking. What does it say?

Sit quietly, letting your child-self stay in your body. Relax.
Open your eyes slowly.

Meditation 4: Becoming More Aware of Your Senses

> When we are collecting information the most significant specific is often
> caught in the corner of our eye.
>
> —DONALD MURRAY

Use this meditation anytime you are writing and you want to
enrich your descriptive language.

Begin by getting comfortable. You can sit in a chair or lie
on the floor.

RELAX FIVE TO TEN SECONDS.

Choose a spot in the room to gaze at. Let your eyes softly focus on that spot, and let the rest of the room just fade away. RELAX FIVE TO TEN SECONDS.

Let your eyelids get heavier and heavier until they close. Feel warm and relaxed. Let your ears take over. Listen carefully to all the sounds that you can hear inside and outside the room. What sounds did you hear when you were a child at home? RELAX TEN TO FIFTEEN SECONDS.

Now become aware of all the things touching you, such as the seat of your chair and your clothes. Feel the way your clothes touch your skin. What do you remember touching as a child when you went to bed, attended school, or played at home? RELAX TEN TO FIFTEEN SECONDS.

And now become aware of the smells in your childhood room, the tastes in your child-mouth. What did you eat for breakfast then? What did you smell when you were a child? RELAX TEN TO FIFTEEN SECONDS.

Now become aware of the inside of your skin, how your bones and the inside of your body touch your skin. How did they touch your skin when you were a child? RELAX TEN SECONDS.

When you are ready, come back. Become aware again of the place where you began this meditation. Take a deep breath, and feel rested and alert.

BUILDING A MEMORY INVENTORY

> What a release to write so that one forgets one's companion, forgets where one is or what one is going to do next.
>
> —ANNE MORROW LINDBERGH

Now that meditation has helped you to find and reexperience some of your memories, you are ready to write them down in thematic memory lists. Taken together, these lists will become your Memory Inventory. Later you will examine, explore, and develop these lists. The exercises here are designed to help you find your themes. Between my suggestions and your own ideas, you will probably generate many more memories than you will actually be able to use. But generating an abundance of memories will enable you to choose the best ideas out of many.

If you are having trouble remembering, here are four things you can do:

1. Throughout this book are samples of writing contributed by myself, my students, colleagues, family, friends, and professional writers. In this section are sample memory lists. Read them over for ideas. Other writers' memories may stimulate yours.
2. Look at photographs from your childhood while you meditate, or talk with family members to see what they remember about you.
3. Imagine instead of remembering. Memory and imagination are intertwined and stored in the same place in your brain. Using one often stimulates the other.
4. Pick a childhood scene that you remember and look at it from various vantage points: from your own, from that of the other people in the scene, from an airplane, from the perspective of a stranger. Remember what you felt about the scene and what you feel about it now.

Find a comfortable spot to sit in. Do not forget to bring your memory notebook and pen or pens. Create a separate section in your notebook titled "Memory Inventory." Use at least one page for each list, reserving some blank pages for the childhood events that you may remember at another time and want to list.

Memory List 1: Distractions

Writing down what keeps you from remembering helps you to empty your mind of those distractions so that you can focus on your childhood memories.

In the left-hand column of your notebook, list the distractions in the present that get in the way of your remembering.

Sample

Present: my aching shoulder, an itch on my nose, the telephone
ringing in the other room, the cat wanting to be let out.
Future: what I am going to cook for dinner tonight, my
father's birthday next week, my blood test tomorrow, my
dental appointment, the phone calls I have to return, a
meeting with a client, money problems.

JUNE GOULD

In the *right-hand column,* begin your *Process Journal.* Prioritize the things that distracted you from remembering. What is
your most pressing distraction? Is it something that can and
should be taken care of before you write? If so, do it and get it
over with. If not, ask yourself if you are using the distraction as
an excuse to keep from remembering. Make a note to yourself
about when you will actually take care of this concern.

Memory List 2: Landmark Events

The world is not what I think but what I live through.
—MAURICE MERLEAU-PONTY

Landmark events are important, once-in-a-lifetime events and
first-time events that everyone experiences. Once-in-a-lifetime
events include funerals and religious events, such as baptisms,
christenings, bar and bat mitzvahs, confirmations, and so on.
First-time events include first days of school, first haircut, first
dental appointment, first lost tooth, first bike ride, first roller
skates, first ice skates, as well as the first time you got lost,
went somewhere by yourself, went to a movie, watched TV,
petted an animal, remembered a dream, got a baseball mitt,
played basketball, tried a new food, became aware of your sex-
uality, broke a bone, got an award, failed or got good grades

on a report card, played ball, swam, got in a fight, and so on.

Do Meditation 2, "Tapping into the Stream," before beginning this exercise. Sit in a comfortable spot and let the meditation and the two sample lists that follow trigger your memories. As they come to the surface, write down your own list of landmark events in the left-hand column of your notebook.

Samples

Dancing in the conga line at my aunt Sylvia's wedding.

Walking home from school myself but I got lost, didn't cry until I got home.

Dr. Friedlander's pulling out my tooth and giving me laughing gas, which made me see and hear monsters.

Spanking I got for saying "shut up" to Mother, cried in bathroom.

Sailing newspaper boats in my grandmother's bathtub with my cousin Harvey.

Climbing to the top of the monkey bars and spitting down through the bars to the asphalt.

JUNE GOULD

Knowing my father had left when I saw his empty closet.

Wearing an angel costume and running up and down the stairs in wings.

Liking to be sick because I could read in bed.

Going to Camp Ramapo and crying into my pillow.

Wetting my pants in day care and being sent home.

Being sent to another class on the first day of school because I could read, I felt rejected.

HELENE FAGIN, psychoanalyst

Memory List 3: Finding Your Childhood Voice

What would happen if one woman told the truth about her life? The world would split open.

—KÄTHE KOLLWITZ

Getting in touch with your child-self helps you to hear what
your original, authentic voice sounded like before it was sub-
merged. It also stimulates your ability to remember. Use this exercise when you want to get in touch with your childhood voice.

Do Meditation 3, "Finding Your Childhood Voice," before
doing this exercise. After meditating, take hold of your child-
self. Imagine he or she is sitting on your lap holding your pen.
Let her or him write a list of school memories in the left-hand
column of your notebook.

Sample

School smelled bad.
Had to sit in hall as a punishment.
Didn't like school.
Loved my metal lunch box, which was rough gray outside,
    smooth white inside.
Lunch box smelled good, like metal, sandwiches, milk, wax
    paper, cold, and home.
When I stood in line, I banged my lunch box against my
    leg.
Moved my leg back and forth every time I stood in line
    because it felt good.

JIM WHEELER, *artist, art teacher*

In the right-hand column of your Process Journal, write what
it felt like to let your childhood voice out. Here is Jim Wheeler's
account of what it felt like to write the preceding selection.

Sample

It felt wonderful. I hadn't thought of that lunch box in
thirty-five years, and yet there it was, and I tell you, I could
smell it just like I was holding it in my hand right then
when I was writing. The incredible thing is that it led to
more memories. I'd like to write about my mother's kitchen

now, where she packed all our lunch boxes. I can see that kitchen so clearly, the beige enameled metal table with the end leaves that would pop down and slide under the top; the linoleum floor, our two refrigerators and on top of one, the Hallicrafter TV, with a screen so small that you had to squint and crane your neck in order to join the world of "I Remember Mama" or "Texaco Star Theater."

Memory List 4: Using Your Senses

To describe our growing up in the lowcountry of South Carolina, I would have to take you to the marsh on a spring day, flush the great blue heron from its silent occupation, scatter marsh hens as we sink to our knees in mud, open you an oyster with a pocketknife and feed it to you from the shell and say, "There. That taste. That's the taste of my childhood." I would say, "Breathe deeply," and you would breathe and remember that smell for the rest of your life.

—PAT CONROY

Expressing what you hear, taste, smell, feel, and see when you write helps your readers empathize with you and experience their own emotions.

Relax and get in touch with your senses—do Meditation 4, "Becoming More Aware of Your Senses," before you begin this exercise. In the left-hand column of your notebook, list some of the things you can hear, touch, feel, taste, and smell right now in your present life. Use the sample lists as springboards, if you like.

Sample

Hear: the sound of my computer humming, the Merritt Parkway, the sound of cars, birds, my lawn being mowed, my own breathing, the venetian blind fluttering against the window, my heart beating.

Touch: my crepe skirt, silk blouse, nylon stockings, leather

shoes, computer keyboard, the backs of my hands, my wedding ring.
Feel: bones running down my arms and legs, my backbone
arching over my lungs and kidneys, my teeth, my shoes.
Taste: my breakfast bran muffin, grapefruit, black coffee,
calcium pills, ice water.
Smell: coffee, my perfume, the cut grass.

JUNE GOULD

In the right-hand column continue your Process Journal.
List some of the things you heard, touched, tasted, and smelled
as a child.

WORDS RISING (excerpt)

I open my journal, write a few
sounds with green ink, and
suddenly
fierceness enters me, stars
begin to revolve, and pick up
alligator dust from under the
ocean.
The music comes. I feel the bushy
tail of the Great Bear
reach down and brush the sea
floor.

—ROBERT BLY

Memory List 5: People, Places, and Things

Everyone looks in front of him; as for me, I look inside of me; I have
no business but with myself; I continually observe myself, I take stock
of myself, I taste myself.

—MONTAIGNE

Generalities bore; specifics fascinate. Focusing on the specific people, places, and things in your childhood will pull your reader into your writing.

Do Meditation 2, "Tapping into the Stream," before doing this exercise. In the left-hand column of your notebook, list some important people, places, and things from your childhood. Use the following sample lists to help you generate your own list, if you like.

Sample

People: Helen Baine, my best friend; Dr. Baine, her father; my mother, Leah; my father, Abraham; my sister, Sylvia; and my brothers, Morris, David, and Eddy; the Indian women who nursed their children on the steps of my father's grocery store in La Tuque, Quebec; my teacher, Miss Cash, who gave me an end-of-school present.

Places: the flats where I picked mayflowers for my teachers; Duncan Avenue, where I lived when we moved to Ontario; Helen Baine's playroom with more books and toys than I had ever seen; my house on the Sabbath lit with candles and smelling of baked bread; my father's grocery store with the penny candy in jars; the scary room in the basement of the convent where I practiced the piano, I thought the big bass fiddle in the corner was a dead body.

Things: my threadbare coat that was too cold in the winter; my brother's bike, he got one but I never did because I was a girl; our Model T Ford with the isinglass curtains; my mother's gold chain; my gold earrings that I think my mother sold to buy herself a ring (I have the ring now); the hand-me-down fur-collared coat that someone offered to my mother for me but which she was too proud to take. (I still want it.)

ETHEL ISRAELSKY, *retired secretary*

Read over your people, places, and things list and choose the most intriguing memory from each list. In the right-hand

column of your notebook, prioritize these three memories according to how much you would like to explore them further in
writing.

These rehearsal activities generate a lot of material, probably
more than you can use for a single piece of writing, or even for
all the exercises in this book. How are you going to begin to sort
through this vast inventory? This is the subject of Chapter 4.

4

Prewriting: Building a Universe

In language, in religion, in art, in science, [we]
can do no more than to build up [our] own
universe—a symbolic universe that enables [us] to
understand and interpret, to articulate and
organize, to synthesize and universalize our
human experience.

—ERNST CASSIRER

Writing calls on two very different skills that can conflict: creating and criticizing. Sometimes these two skills work together, and you get imaginative as well as sharp and well-ordered writing. But usually it is best to separate the creating and criticizing processes so that they do not interfere with each other.

This chapter is designed to help you focus on the creative aspects of your writing. It is important for you to get your critical writing teacher off your shoulder. If you are trying to be inventive, it is terrible to have someone—even your own critical self—come along and tell you that what you are doing is bad, does not make sense, or is dumb. If you want to develop your writing, at this early stage you must push that critic aside and accept the good, the bad, and the pointless. Only when you can accept all your writing attempts will you be able to decide what to keep or what to scrap.

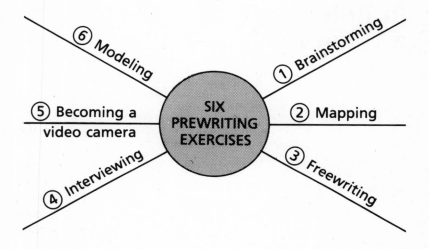

In the six prewriting exercises that follow, I will be encouraging you to be creative, to go out on limbs, without worrying if your words are perfect. The exercises are meant to

- help you see what you have to work with
- loosen you up so that you can expand and extend your original idea
- show you the additional information you may need in order to proceed
- help you make connections with the past and present
- lead you to your voice
- develop your writing fluency

You will need your notebook and pen or pens for this exercise, as well as your Memory Inventory. Do one or more of your favorite meditations. Allow ten minutes for each prewriting exercise.

Use these exercises anytime during your writing process when you feel stuck about a particular idea, image, or memory and want to develop it further.

PREWRITING 1: BRAINSTORMING

No one remains quite what he was when he recognizes himself.
—THOMAS MANN

Brainstorming is list making, the foundation of your writing and thinking processes. Use brainstorming to develop topics, as you did in your Memory Inventory, but also to generate topic-related information. Brainstorming goes by several other names: associational thinking, free association, and link thinking, among others.

Turn to your Memory List 2, "Landmark Events," and choose a pleasant memory that you would like to explore further. Select one of the meditations to relax you and get you into a remembering mood. In the left-hand column of your notebook, write in list form—*single words or phrases*—everything that comes to mind about the landmark event you have chosen. Let one word or phrase remind you of another until you run out of either time or associations.

Sample

APPLE CHUCKERS

Taught brother how to throw a chucker
Ran with him to our orchard
Told my brother not to tell our sisters, they would tattle
Thought I could throw them a mile

Beat the grass down into a path to the orchard
Locusts were humming
Suckers were best because they were springy
Suckers grew out of the sides of fat limbs
Had to twist to get it off tree
Climbed apple tree
Shimmied over limb to get apple suckers
Mother called us to do chores but we were busy hitting the
    center of the hood on George's old De Soto car with
    apples
Swish, swish, kaboom, splat, Bam, swish, crash
Applesauce all over a windshield.

                                              JIM WHEELER

Look back at your brainstorm list and reflect on it. What
is special about a pleasant memory? Why did you choose that
memory in particular? Write your reflections in your Process
Journal, in the right-hand column of your notebook.

Jim Wheeler used his Apple Chuckers brainstorm list as the
basis of the following entry in his Process Journal.

Sample

Teaching my brother how to chuck apples engaged every
part of me when I was a child. My whole body and all of
my senses were involved in this memory: I walked and ran
through the grass, I saw the path my feet made, I smelled
the grass, the apples, the bark of the tree on the limb where
I sat. I felt my muscles flex and tense as I climbed the
tree, and again when I catapulted those apples into the
blue sky, and I also felt my penknife, the apples, and
the pliant sucker branches. I heard birds, locusts, the sounds
of my brother's and mother's voices. I guess it was a moment
where I was thoroughly there, present in time, totally connected to what I was doing. When I think about it now, I
reexperience the pleasure I felt just being alive, and that is
delightful.

PREWRITING 2: MAPPING

> We are here to witness. There is nothing else to do with those mute
> materials we do not need. . . . All we can do with the whole human
> array is watch it.
>
> —ANNIE DILLARD

Mapping is a nonlinear brainstorming process. It is similar to
linear list making except that it allows associations to flow out
and encourages the emergence of themes and patterns. It accepts
mistakes, strange associations, and apparent meandering, so it
encourages startlingly original perceptions and creative connection making.

There are four benefits to mapping:

1. Your original memory becomes more sharply defined.
2. The relative importance of each memory connected to a
   theme is clearly indicated. More important memories are
   closer to the center, and less important ideas are near the edge.
3. The links between memories and between key themes are
   immediately recognizable because of their proximity and connection.
4. The nature of the structure allows for easy additions of new
   information.

These are the steps in making a map of a school-related memory. First do Meditation 3, "Finding Your Childhood Voice."
Then choose an image or person from your Memory Inventory
that you would like to explore further. This image or person
should have to do with school. Write the name of the subject
you want to explore in the center of a circle drawn in your
notebook. Be sure to print in capital letters for legibility. As
ideas about this subject occur to you, draw lines from the center
circle. The lines will branch off and allow you to capture and connect the fragments of information that you have in your memory.

After you have finished your map, look it over. What con-

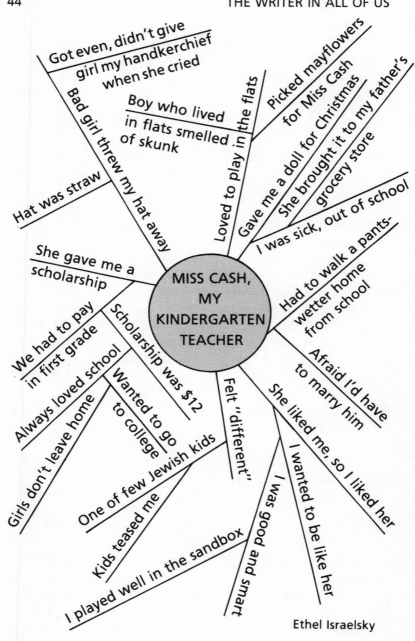

Got even, didn't give girl my handkerchief when she cried

Boy who lived in flats smelled of skunk

Bad girl threw my hat away

Hat was straw

She gave me a scholarship

We had to pay in first grade

Scholarship was $12

Always loved school

Girls don't leave home

Wanted to go to college

One of few Jewish kids

Kids teased me

I played well in the sandbox

I was good and smart

Felt "different"

I wanted to be like her

She liked me, so I liked her

Afraid I'd have to marry him

Had to walk a pants-wetter home from school

I was sick, out of school

She brought it to my father's grocery store

Gave me a doll for Christmas

Picked mayflowers for Miss Cash

Loved to play in the flats

MISS CASH, MY KINDERGARTEN TEACHER

Ethel Israelsky

nections or associations did you make that surprise you? What patterns emerged from it? Prioritize in list form what you would actually include in a written narrative about this memory. Is there anything you forgot? Is there anything you would leave out?

Here is how Ethel Israelsky reflected on her associations and surprises in her mapping experience.

Sample

It felt good to see one of my memories connect to so many others. I wish I could have stretched the sides of my journal to give myself more room for more associations. I was surprised that I remembered the boy who lived in the flats. I always thought he smelled from skunks. His father was a trapper and he skinned and sold animal skins. He must have smelled of those skins. I was also surprised that I remembered an argument with a girl in my class over my straw summer hat; she pulled it off my head and threw it to her friends, but I got even with her by refusing to give her my handkerchief when she cried in school.

After studying the map, Ethel saw the following patterns emerge:

Sample

How much I loved and still love and respect schooling
How deeply different I felt from the other children because I was one of a handful of Jewish children in a predominately French Canadian Catholic community
How much I resented being a girl and not being given the opportunity to go on to higher education; in my day girls were not sent out of town to college, it was not considered proper
How there was a pecking order of discrimination, and the people of the flats were the lowest on the discriminatory totem pole

Ethel went on to prioritize what she would include in a written narrative:

Sample

MY PRIORITY LIST

I would write about my school memory in this order:
1. what school was like and how it had both good and bad parts
The good parts were
a. my teacher Miss Cash, what she looked like and how much she liked me
b. the scholarship I won to go to first grade for free
c. the nice dresses my mother made me and the hats I wore in spring
d. how much I liked to play in the sandbox and run around the flats during recess
The bad parts were
a. how the kids teased me because I was different
b. how much I wanted to continue school later on but girls didn't go away from home to go to college from our community
c. how I had to take a little boy home from school every day because he lived near my house and I was afraid that I would have to marry him when I grew up

Finally Ethel decided what to omit and what to add.

Sample

What I would leave out
a. the part about the boy and smelling of skunk
What I would like to add or know more about
a. I would like to make another map to find out more about the other people who lived in the flats

PREWRITING 3: FREEWRITING

> Every artist preserves deep within him a single source from which, throughout his lifetime, he draws what he is and what he says and when the source dries up the work withers and crumbles.
>
> —ALBERT CAMUS

The term *freewriting* was invented by writing theorist and practitioner Peter Elbow, author of *Writing with Power*. Freewriting forces us to write quickly and fluently without worrying about punctuation, spelling, or making complete sense. By pushing us to dive beneath our surface thoughts, freewriting takes us to the source of our fluency, voice, center of interest, and to the repeating patterns and themes embedded in our memories.

Peter Elbow says that sometimes when you freewrite, you will produce terrible junk. However the goal is for you to expand your brainstorming and mapping memories into extended thoughts. There are benefits to be gained from freewriting: It helps you put extended thoughts and sentences down on paper. It helps you bypass concerns about whether your words sound good or bad. It urges you to write fluently even when you may not feel like it. And finally, it shows you the positive side of pushing yourself toward a deadline.

To begin freewriting, turn to Memory List 4, "Using Your Senses," and choose a sensory memory to expand on. Do Meditation 4, "Becoming More Aware of Your Senses," before you start. Write as fast as you can in the left-hand column of your notebook for ten minutes. Do not worry about punctuation, making sense, or grammar. Don't force your words; just let them flow like a meandering river creating its main bed as well as its tributaries.

Unrelated things—such as fears, obsessions, or current images—may flow out of your pen. If so, just let them, but if you go too far afield, consciously steer yourself back to your main thoughts and images.

You may stop and find you cannot think of anything more

to write. If this happens, do not try to be logical about the next sentence or phrase. Just repeat the last word that you did write, or even any word that comes to mind. For example: *Comes to mind, mind, mind.* . . . *I can't think, think, think.* . . . Repeat the last word until an image, memory, scene, or conversation comes to your mind and through your pen that you can write about.

Samples

BROWN VELVET (excerpt)

"Blue velvet," a song, a pretty song, blue eyes, other little girls had them and blue dresses—light blue, feminine, young. "Brown velvet," browner than velvet, velvet, were her eyes, softer than May her gentle sighs, no, no, velvet, brown velvet, my mother's wedding dress was blue velvet, and slim and sculptured, yet soft, not much else was velvet in my young life, until the hat, the brown velvet hat, it was soft, yet sculptured, sculptured, I remember its lining was quilted silk, so lustrous it was almost iridescent, and that was only the lining! Outside was the real show, velvet *and* fur, not the lumpy Persian lamb fur on my mother's shoulder next to me in church, but the smooth mink fur on the stout lady's back three rows in front, front.

Oh, I remember, I could stroke the fur in one direction and it would look one way and then run my fingers back the other way and it would change again. Just like something else, what, what, something gold, gold, I know, the antique velvet on Aunt Margaret's couch. She had good taste, antique gold velvet and I was allowed to sit there, running my fingers, even palms, over the cushions next to me, making more elaborate patterns when the adult talk became too boring, boring, but so what boring, her whole house was "velvet," it had everything—even a rumpus room where we kids could go and eat, whole jars of smooth, sweet, red maraschino cherries. Down there

I'd sit on red leather bar stools, or red leather built-in banquet cushions that creaked as I rocked.

MARY WINSKY, *teacher*

THE SOLDIER UNIFORM

Friends, relatives, people, lots of people, kids my own age. The house was white and the back porch was gray and small with a white railing around it. And you had to pass sideways, sideways . . . a screen door that banged out the rhythm of in and out . . . in and out . . . in, in . . . out . . . out . . . out . . . in. The sound of in is always different from the sound of out. I was there, there, there, on that day I grabbed the jacket off the doorknob as I dashed for the backseat of the car. How grand it was—that jacket. Khaki with dark brown belt and brass buttons and the cap with a brim that went with it. I knew without talking about it, because one never talked of such things, that when I wore it I was taken for a man. A grownup man. Sort of like pretending to read so everyone would marvel—"look at him read."

The day must have passed that way on parade, parade, I don't remember, remember, soldier. "Oh, look at him, doesn't he look just like a soldier?" The faces are gone, the conversations are gone, also the games, the ride there and the ride home, gone too is that jacket and its accompanying hat, but the reaction to the comments, the feeling of belonging, the never to be expressed desire to be noticed have stayed with me today, symbolized, contained, woven into the very fabric of that jacket—khaki with brass buttons down the front and on the pockets. The cardboard made to look like leather, the belt and the hat with a bill to match.

JIM WHEELER

After you have freewritten for ten minutes, stop and ask yourself these questions. What did it feel like to write without censoring yourself? Could you do it freely? What came out of your freewriting that surprised you? What image, thought, or memory would you like to pursue? Circle the part of your freewriting that you like best. Answer these questions in your Process Journal as Mary Winsky and Jim Wheeler have done.

Samples

I was sitting on a blue velvet couch when I started the piece and it was as though that couch triggered all the velvet associations. I want to pursue the brown velvet hat because I lost it in the B. Altman department store in New York and I cried over it because I loved it so much. The line I liked best was "I could stroke the fur in one direction and it would look one way and then run my fingers back the other way and it would change again."

MARY WINSKY

I liked writing and remembering and just letting it flow out. I haven't thought about that soldier suit in thirty-five years but there it was coming out of my pen. I was surprised that I remembered how grown up I felt and how wearing that suit was like pretending to read. I would like to pursue that house and the family parties we had there. We lived there a very short time. The part I liked best was "the cardboard made to look like leather, the belt and the hat with a bill to match."

JIM WHEELER

PREWRITING 4: INTERVIEWING

Interviewing is a basic tool that writers use to get information for their plays, novels, poems, research papers, and reports. You, however, will use interviews to help attune yourself to your creativity and recall childhood memories. These interviews may be real or imagined; you may interview not only persons but places and objects in your imagination.

Draw on your Memory List 5, "People, Places, and Things," as a resource for this exercise. Based on that list, choose a person, place, or object to interview. If you choose to interview a real person, write down the questions you wish to ask him or her in advance. Be sure to ask questions that your readers would like to have answered as well as your own. You will want to ask your interviewee questions about your childhood.

Use a tape recorder or take notes so that you get the interviewee's actual words. While your interviewee answers your questions, listen for the gifts and surprises embedded in the stories. Conduct the interview face-to-face if possible so that you can notice body language and facial expression. Afterward, write down the interview in the left-hand column of your notebook.

If the person you want to interview has died, moved away, or simply disappeared from your current location, conduct an imaginary interview with him or her.

Samples

INTERVIEW WITH A PERSON: MY AUNT ETHEL

LESLIE: What is your first memory of me?

ETHEL: I remember coming to see you when you were a newborn baby. We stayed with your mother and father in their first apartment on Government Road. Your mother was giving you a bath. You had both arms behind you scratching your back. You had eczema. Where did you get it? Nobody in our family was allergic. We found out your grandmother was allergic.

LESLIE: What was I like at school age?

ETHEL: I have pictures of you when you started school, in your plaid skirt. You used to send me cards with buttons stuck on. You wrote, "Ha ha, I can spell."

I used to tell you that your eyes lit up when you smiled. You had shiny black, beautiful hair. Your mother brushed and combed you.

LESLIE: What were some of my other qualities?

ETHEL: You were close to your mother. You were strong willed. Your father would yell at you and you would yell back. Your chin would stick out just like his. When you got older you were bossy. You bossed the maid.

LESLIE: What did you think I liked to do best?

ETHEL: You loved to read and you would have your nose in a book, even when you were very little.

LESLIE: Do you remember anything about my relationship with my brother, Rick?

ETHEL: When we visited in the summer, we slept on the porch— funny bedroom! The milkman came in and delivered the milk. You and Rick used to peek over and look through the window to see if we were awake. I would see your faces and fingernails. When I saw your eyes peering at us I would say, "Lou, don't move!"

LESLIE MILLS, *teacher*

INTERVIEW WITH A PLACE: MY BROOKLYN LOBBY

JUNE: I remember you. You're the lobby in our apartment building that I always returned to after school. Why have I remembered you now? What do you have to tell me about my childhood?

LOBBY: I have nothing to tell you. Simply recall me, enter me once more, and be awed, impressed, chilled by my grandeur.

JUNE: What an awful thing to say. You said this to me when I was a child too. I wanted to be welcomed when I came home from school, not overwhelmed by cold grandeur.

LOBBY: But I breathe space. I was meant to give you some idea of the largeness of the universe! Don't you like my high ceilings?

JUNE: No. I don't feel I am breathing space when I enter you. I feel you are pulling me into your image and I must breathe to your rhythms and design. You don't meet me halfway.

LOBBY: I don't have to care about what you think. I was designed by an architect. I have black-and-white marble floors, a stained-glass window, and a Moorish table and chairs. And what do you think of my simulated-concrete wall blocks? Don't you think they look like they're from the Sphinx or from the Egyptian pyramids? Don't they remind you of the ancient, the inscrutable, the miracle of simulation?

JUNE: Why couldn't your walls have been plain like me?

LOBBY: You were not so plain. You were as grand and complex as I was. You just couldn't see that when you were a child. I gave you something to aspire to. How would you have ever known there was a bigger, more elegant outside world than the small three-room apartment you lived in? It's the contrast, the conflict with my fabulous size and your cramped quarters that made you want to be independent, to write, to grow, to leave. Looking back at me now in this interview helps you to realize that in my own peculiar way I helped you expand your horizons and flex your imagination.

JUNE GOULD

INTERVIEW WITH AN OBJECT: PINKY, MY BLANKET

LIZ: I remember you, you're the blanket I used to call Pinky. What did you mean to me when I was little?

PINKY: You needed me when you felt insecure. I nestled in your arms when you were a child. I kept you from the scary creatures you imagined were hiding in your attic.

LIZ: I remember now, I always thought the wind in the attic sounded like a ghost moaning. I used to cuddle up with you and rub your corner against my cheek. You helped me feel safe.

PINKY: Do you remember my crocheted bumps? Can you see my diamond-shaped design? Can't you still smell my fresh Ivory soap aroma when I came to you hot out of the washing machine?

LIZ: Yes, and even now, when I feel scared about school, going away to camp, or trying something new like tap dancing, I can see you in my mind's eye and I feel better. I will never forget you, Pinky, and I will give a blanket like you to my children someday.

ELIZABETH GOULD, *age* 12

After you have written down your interview, ask yourself what you learned about your childhood that you did not know before. Write it down in your Process Journal.

Samples

Here is what Leslie wrote about her interview with a person:

> I remembered everything that my Aunt Ethel told me because I've heard those stories before but I loved hearing them again. The interview helped me get in touch with the way I was back then. I liked myself, especially the part where my eyes were shining!

Here is what June wrote about interviewing a place:

> I only had negative memories about my Brooklyn lobby before I wrote this interview. Now I realize that the lobby did have its positive points. I also remember that I was afraid of it because it was so large and so different than any of the other spaces that I inhabited as a child.

Here is what Elizabeth wrote about interviewing her blanket:

> I realize that it has been a long time since I felt scared at night. Pinky was an important part of my life and if I misplaced it or my mother washed it I missed it and wanted it back. I can feel how I felt then just thinking about it now.

PREWRITING 5: BECOMING A VIDEO CAMERA

Without memory, a person would not have the sense of continuity even to know who he or she was. Without a doubt, memory is central to being human.

—ELIZABETH LOFTUS

A video camera drinks everything in without editing. Imagine that you are a video camera and can do that too. You zoom in and out, move close to and far away from your subject. You approach from an angle and focus on a particular detail. But you remain totally open to everything that happens, just reporting what you see as you point yourself at the objects and people in your past. Later you can cut and splice, edit the film, and make it mean something, but the first stage is to take it all in.

Writing researcher Donald Murray says that "the writer is always *receiving revealing details* [such as] the way one teacher carries a pile of books to class and builds a little wall of books between himself and his students, the way another teacher uses the latest campus slang in precisely the wrong way." When you become a video camera, you will be able to store up this kind of revealing detail about people, places, and things from your past.

Choose a place to videotape from your Memory List 5, "People, Places, and Things." As you videotape in your imagination, you will also see people whom you know inhabit that place. Record, in list form, phrases about what you see through your camera in the left-hand column of your notebook. List the revealing details about people, places, and things.

Samples

It's the corner of Lincoln Road and Flatbush Avenue in Brooklyn. Miss Leona Tunick is sitting on the corner on a milk box. She's saying hello to me and calling me Joannie, Jeannie, Janie . . . everything but June. This is nothing new.

She has whiskers coming out of her chin. She's asking me to buy a quart of milk for her and to pick up the newspaper, the *Brooklyn Eagle*. I feel she's been waiting especially for me to run an errand for her.

She is leaning against Reiter's Drug Store window, which not only has a "Breck Girl" poster but a tan plastic leg with an Ace bandage wrapped around its knee. There are dead flies scattered around the window's interior ledge and a Revlon poster advertising Cherries in the Snow lipstick.

I look down at Miss Tunick's twisted legs which are encased in high, black leather, buttoned shoes. Her crutches are leaning against the yellow-brown brick of our apartment house.

I see an olive green mailbox and fire hydrant on the corner, a maple tree, wire-mesh wastepaper basket, and a sewer grate stuffed with papers in the gutter.

My friends Roberta Kendall and Marion Weiss are taking turns throwing a skate key into the numbered boxes of our hopscotch game.

There's my father stepping up onto the curb at the corner, I see his bald head, mustache, white, short-sleeved shirt, Chesterfield cigarettes stuck into his shirt pocket, tan gabardine pleated slacks, he's carrying the PM newspaper under his arm, I run to him and as he bends over to hug me I feel his mustache bristle against my cheek. . . .

JUNE GOULD

THE BIG ROCKS

This is my neighborhood in the Bronx. I'm across the street from my house, where there is a big rock formation we call The Alley. It's shaped like a triangle and made of huge black rocks, boulders really, some stretching ten feet high.

Kids are climbing all over them, they are hiding their hidden treasures in the rocks' crevices so their mothers won't find them. I see them hiding sticks, tires, cartons, cans, cages, cigarettes . . .

It is swampy, I see myself catching frogs. I keep my animal collections and jars of ants here.

I am also catching a squirrel with Leslie and Steven. Steven is wearing dungarees and a white T-shirt. Leslie is wearing penny loafers, jeans, and a big, wide, black belt and white T-shirt. We all have crew cuts.

We're climbing and taking care of our squirrel by feeding it leaves and nuts. I can see through the chicken wire we used to make a cage.

KENNETH TEWEL, *professor of school administration,*
Queens College

Read over the revealing details that you discovered about the people, places, and things in your video recording. Write connecting statements about your childhood in your Process Journal.

Samples

Revealing Details: Miss Tunick, whiskers, twisted legs, crutches
My father, bald head, mustache, the paper under his arm
Connecting Statement: I feel guilty when I say no to someone, but I resent it when someone manipulates me to do something for them when I would rather not comply. Typically, though, I give in because I hate confrontations.

JUNE GOULD

Revealing Details: Leslie, Steven and me; crew cuts, jeans, penny loafers, black belt, T-shirts
Connecting Statement: The world seemed to belong to everyone except the kids, but here at the rocks I could forget about the rules that applied to the rest of the world.

KENNETH TEWEL

PREWRITING 6: MODELING

Successful writers often say that they learned their craft by copying other writers. They do not mean that they plagiarized other writers' ideas or actual words. They mean that they gave themselves the liberty to imitate compelling sentence structure, tone, style, and voice. By using someone else's writing as a model to express yourself, you will develop a storehouse of writing frameworks that you can call on and use as needed.

For this exercise, select and do your favorite meditation before writing. Choose a member of your family to write about. Read the following list-poem. Notice the poet's construction of phrases, the tone of her reminiscences, and the concept of listing objects to describe the person. Copy these characteristics as you write your own list-poem in the left-hand column of your notebook, listing the person's most important personal effects, tangible and intangible. Finally, make a closing statement about the essence of your person's life.

PERSONAL EFFECTS

One lady's
handbag, containing
rosary beads, elevated
railroad ticket, small pin
with picture, pocket knife,
one small purse containing
$1.68 in cash,
handkerchiefs,
a small mirror, a pair of gloves,
two thimbles, a Spanish
comb, one yellow metal ring,
five keys, one
fancy glove button,
one lady's handbag containing
one gent's watch case
number of movement 6418593
and a $1 bill,
one half dozen postal cards,
a buttonhook, a man's photo,
a man's garter,
a razor strap,
one portion of limb and hair
of human being.

—MARY FELL

Sample

MY GRANDMOTHER'S TRUNK

A bottle of port wine, a little wineglass,
Tintypes of Ireland,
a good black fringed shawl,
a lock of hair,
a man's gold pocket watch,
"good" bone combs,
fancy little embroidered table runners,
dark silk dresses,
a cedar smell mixed with mothballs,
old button-up black shoes,
a chunk of peat with a green bow tied around it,
Irish stories about hard work on the farm,
a thatched-roof house overlooking a lake,
flowered teacups,
a private domain in my mother's house
entered only at my grandmother's
invitation.

     MARY T. SHEERIN, *core professor, Union Graduate School*

Here is an excerpt from a prose poem written by a professional poet. You may use it as a model to write a food poem yourself.

My mother, my grandmother sit at the white enamel kitchen table, kneading dough, shelling peas, measuring pine nuts into the chopped lamb and onions, soaking the crushed wheat for kibbeh, filling dozens of meat pies, stuffing chicken and squash and green peppers and eggplant, rolling stuffed grape leaves and stuffed cabbage like cigars, making dumplings for yoghurt soup among cans of sesame oil and boiled butter, peeling scores of potatoes for baked lamb necks and shanks and roast chicken, boiling rice, browning rice and onions, adding rice and tomatoes to large pots of marrow-bone vegetable soup, sitting and chatting over familiar tasks that are done must be done will be done every day without respite, my mother, my grandmother at the kitchen table with me between them on a stool in the corner where I watch and listen, tasting dough and stuffing, rewards for being content to observe and accept, with my silence, their love.

—D. H. MELHEM

Questions Students Ask About Prewriting

Should I do all the prewriting exercises before I write?
You can use all of them if you want to, but that is not essential. What is important now is to learn them. Experience each exercise so that you can call on the one or ones that will be most helpful to you when needed.

Are prewriting exercises meant to be used only before I actually begin writing?
Use prewriting exercises at any stage of your writing process. They will help you to focus on details, expand your topic, sequence your thoughts, and construct meanings.

Doesn't prewriting take a lot of time away from my actual writing?
The time it takes to prewrite is well spent because it helps you avoid blank-page syndrome, which can sometimes take years to overcome. It also clarifies your thinking so that you need to spend less time revising.

Why can't I outline instead of using all these exercises? It seems much quicker, and less complicated, and less time-consuming.
Outlining is linear and forces you to invent a finished design for your writing before your thoughts have been discovered and crystallized. Use an outline only after you are almost finished revising; it will help you to see fragments that you may be missing. Some people can use an outline without feeling they are stuck with a preordained design. If you are one of these people, continue to use it; if not, the prewriting exercises will ultimately prove more fruitful.

Do any of the prewriting exercises ever come out so well that you don't have to revise them?
Sometimes, when the moon and stars are just right and you are in a perfect state of reception, some of the prewriting exercises need little or no revision. It is rare but not im-

possible. Be careful, however, not to get so romantically attached to your first prewriting words that you imagine they are perfect when they are not. The only way to find out if they are any good is to sleep on them and read them to someone whose judgment you trust, or send them out to an appropriate publisher and see what happens.

Why is my prewriting sometimes more interesting and spontaneous than my drafts?

Sometimes we work the life out of prewriting when we revise it. In time, this problem should disappear. Remember to keep yourself open during all stages of your writing process so that your words can flow through you freely. Learn to suspend judgment until the very last draft, in which you tighten up. Don't chop up creative and spontaneous language and images at this point.

Prewriting is the first step in tapping your writing potential. You have tried six prewriting exercises and explored, completed, or organized some of your memories. Now we come to the next task of the writing process: to mold your prewriting ramblings, explorations, and imitations. Chapter 5 will show you how to shape your prewritten memories into focused personal narratives, family stories, portraits, letters, dialogues, and poems.

5

Drafting: Shaping the Chaos

*Generally, the geology of our lives is a layered
mass—a labyrinthed mineshaft of compressed
memory, charred meteors imbedded in brain cells.
Still, in order to write recollectively, these
blackened nodules must be visited. Then, when
contact is made, they must be sensed beyond
personal property and reset within a landscape
whose topography may be traveled by all.*
—HANNELORE HAHN

Drafting is the process of composing the first full version of a
piece of writing. It is somewhat like freewriting in that you let
your words flow freely and fluently onto the page without regard
to punctuation, grammar, spelling, or polish. The difference
between freewriting and drafting is that when you are drafting you have a definite purpose in mind, a storehouse of prewritten material from which to draw, and an organizational plan
to follow.

This chapter will show you how to develop drafts. You will
develop drafts in different genres: *personal narratives, family stories,
portraits, letters, dialogues,* and *poems.* Although there are many
more literary genres—novels, plays, essays, reports, mono-
logues—the six I have chosen can act as springboards to the
others. Experiencing different genres will help you find your own
writing voice, style, and fluency.

The six categories of exercises that follow will help you

shape your memories into a coherent whole with a beginning and an ending. By helping you focus both on the details and on the central themes of your writing, the exercises will help you discover your ultimate writing design. Use these exercises after prewriting, or when you want to shape a memory into a particular genre or category.

You will need your notebook and pen, or pens, your Memory Inventory, and your prewriting exercises. Do one or more of your favorite meditations. Allow twenty minutes or more for each drafting exercise.

PERSONAL NARRATIVES

> The one who believes in God tells Him the story. The one who does not must tell it to progeny, to humankind, and to oneself. Homo narrans, humankind as storyteller, is a human constant.
>
> —BARBARA MYERHOFF

Narratives are stories, the telling of events arranged in time sequence. All the fairy tales of our childhood are narratives; so are myths, operas, soap operas, and most movies. Anthropologist Barbara Myerhoff says that we tell our tales aloud to ourselves "to prove that there is existence, to tame the chaos of the world, to give meaning. The tale certifies the fact of being and gives sense at the same time." The need to tell our stories is as compelling as the need for food, love, sex, and safety.

Narrative 1: An Object

> Writing begins with all that we have known since we were born, and perhaps with a lot of knowledge that was born in us. We write, first of all, to discover what we know and then what we need to know.
>
> —DONALD MURRAY

Choose your favorite meditation to relax you, and do it. Then, from Memory List 5, "People, Places, and Things," choose an object to write about. In the left-hand column of your notebook, tell its story sequentially, giving the story a beginning, middle, and end. Do not leave anything out. Try to include what this childhood object meant to you.

Sample

THE TRUNK (excerpt)

Our apartment was small so the trunk was hidden deep in a closet. My mother and I would first have to remove all the family's clothes from the closet. Then there were boxes of books, linens, shoes, and old papers. The closet was so deep that I felt I would suffocate in it. After the stacks of boxes came more clothes: old coats, my father's double-breasted brown suit and a moth-eaten muskrat coat that my mother was saving. Below these odds and ends rested the trunk.

The inside of the trunk was lined with pink flowered paper. I remember a little drawer that lifted up and out. Folded neatly in this drawer were yards of velvet ribbon, rolls of frilly edging, and a variety of crocheted collars and cuffs. In the trunk stacked layer upon layer were fabric, lace, net, satin, and velvet. There was an iridescent white lace that reminded me of the strands of pearls my grandmother wore. A soft black net frightened me because it looked like the veils worn by mourners. There were remnants of imported lace. Many of these had gold or silver threads woven through them. Some pieces were fragile with intricate patterns; others, more substantial. A beautiful piece of imported white lace had been put aside for a wedding gown, always wrapped carefully in tissue paper; taken out and measured periodically but never used. It still remains in the trunk waiting for a bride.

Sometimes the trunk would be left out for several days. Hour after hour would be spent playing, sorting, touching and fantasizing. I would caress a vivid red lace and imagine a dress I would make out of it: a heart-shaped neckline, short puffed sleeves, and a three-tiered skirt.

PHYLLIS BELLOFATTO, *teacher*

Now think about these questions: What did this story mean to you when it happened? What does it mean to you now, while you are looking back at it? Explore these questions in your Process Journal. Phyllis Bellofatto wrote the following reaction to her memory of the trunk.

Sample

When I was a child and the door to my room was closed, the trunk opened and I entered a new world. Dressed up I felt pretty, exciting, and confident. I had the social graces I lacked in my everyday life. The games I created helped me to survive my mother's silence during her depression and the unreasonable restrictions put on me by overprotective parents.

I seem to be feeling some of the same old emotions now. I need something to make me feel special and excited. I can no longer close my door, dress up, and act out a part, but remembering back to the old trunk, the fabric, and the games makes me feel better. So I talk about starting a new career as a fashion designer. Maybe this time I will open the trunk and find in it a new beginning.

Narrative 2: A Lost Object

The events of childhood do not pass, but repeat themselves like seasons of the year.

—ELEANOR FARJEON

For this exercise, write about something you lost as a child that you still miss or that you remember vividly. This lost object can be money, clothing, jewelry, a book, gloves—anything. If you cannot remember something you actually lost, you may still do this exercise by making up a lost object. How did losing the object make you feel? Describe your emotions and physical sensations at the time. Do this narrative form in the left-hand column of your notebook.

Sample (excerpt)

I threw myself down on the white chenille bedspread. Briefly I thought of how the bumps would mark my cheeks if I didn't turn the spread down but dismissed the fussy thoughts with the warmth of the first tears.

I had held it in so long, for hours really, since the moment I had discovered the brown velvet hat was missing in New York City, to the moment I collapsed on the bed in my suburban room, where I had arrived finally after running through the cold city streets, into the noisy bustle of Grand Central Station, then into the overheated train, then out again into the darkened parking lot coldness, then into the backseat of the family car.

By now the chenille was really wet and warm and bumpier than ever. But I couldn't turn it down now because my fists were clenched so tightly and the sobs were beginning to shake me. I moved the fist to my mouth and bit hard. I thought I'd cry forever and maybe this time I wouldn't even care if they heard me.

But they must not have because I was mercifully allowed to drift off to sleep. But the mercy was brief because the hat was in the dream. This time it was on the head of a brown dog. He was cute and pudgy but he was wearing my hat. I would get it back but as I approached him, his cute, sad face snarled suddenly and the beloved brown velvet hat turned into an army cap, pushed back on the head of a growling bulldog sergeant. No, I'd never get it back.

MARY WINSKY

Look at the first line of your narrative. This is called your *lead line*. A good lead line pulls the reader into your story. Does yours? In your Process Journal, write about your response to your lead line. Mary Winsky wrote this response to hers.

Sample

I like my first line, "I threw myself down on the white chenille bedspread," because I think it piques the readers' interest. When they read that they think, I wonder what caused her to be so unhappy?

Narrative 3: A Landmark Event

The writer should remind himself that there is not and has never been any substitute for emotion. The cold writers turn nothing loose—neither passion nor pain, beauty nor truth.

—PEGGY SIMSON CURRY

Choose a landmark event in your life and, in the left-hand column of your notebook, write a narrative about it. Make use of dialogue.

Sample

THE MORNING AFTER (excerpt)

"I can't come out and play with you, my daddy died last night."

Jill looked doubtfully through the screen door. Her stubby cocker spaniel puppy pulled impatiently at his new, stiff leather leash. "But my mom sent me over to play. You said you wanted to see my new puppy."

I didn't know why but I didn't open the door. I probably should have stepped out into the backyard and explained it all to my friend . . . but I couldn't. I wasn't upset. I just didn't want to open the door.

The cool June morning air blew softly through the screen. Jill was there and her nosy puppy was sniffing around the circumference of his leash in jerky, little movements. But somehow it didn't seem like I should step out and pet him.

"My mom will be mad at me if I come home so soon," Jill whined.

"Just tell her my daddy died last night," I told her again.

"But she won't believe me!" Jill complained. "She'll think I made it up and she'll get mad at me."

"Well it's true," I insisted. She followed my glance inside. My mother was seated next to the insurance man in the living room. They were talking quietly.

"Just ask your mom if I could bring Taffy in, just for a little while."

I hurried quietly up the three linoleum steps into the kitchen. I tried to keep my eyes from looking down at the floor, but against my will they were drawn as if pulled like a magnet.

My mother looked up. "Jill came over to show me her new puppy. She wants to know if you want to see it."

"No, not today, honey." Even my mother's voice sounded weary. "Ask her to come back next week."

My fingers played with the painted wooden border on the screen door as I explained to Jill that she would have to come back some other time.

To get up to my room I would have to go through the kitchen again, so instead I sat down on the cool linoleum steps. Maybe in the dim quiet of the hallway stairs I could think about last night. I rested my chin on my elbows and watched as my elbows made pink marks on my bare knees. Maybe I could figure out what had happened and what was going to happen now.

I decided I hated Jill's new dog.

DONNA SKOLNICK, *teacher*

Read over your draft and look at the ending. It should grow out of the beginning. Does your ending grow out of your beginning, as a tadpole turns into a frog? Or does it get stuck somewhere before it metamorphoses fully? Write your answers to these questions in your Process Journal. Here is Donna Skolnick's succinct response to the questions.

Sample

My beginning and ending tell the story of how my life and my attitude were changed on that tragic day.

FAMILY STORIES

Memories not in me only, but in me through my mother's mother, reaching back beyond her sepia photographs.

—MARC KAMINSKY

Most families unconsciously designate a certain family member as the chronicler of their history. This storyteller helps to pass the experiences of the family down through the generations. Because family stories pass through many lips, ears, and voices, and become polished and embellished in the process, they begin to sound like legends and myths. As succeeding generations tell and interpret them, the stories often become metaphors for the way a family sees itself in the world.

Family stories that are rich in descriptive detail, action, and meaning tie present generations to future ones and thereby transmit family values and culture. Remembering an oft-told family story helps release the natural writer in you.

In the left-hand column of your notebook, write down a family story that was frequently told in your family, especially when you were a child. Write the story to the best of your recollection, but if you have trouble remembering it, tape a member of your family telling the story.

Samples

MY FATHER AND THE RUBBER GALOSHES

When my father first came to Quebec he had to make a living any way he could. He bought used rubber galoshes from French housewives by going door to door and then he sold them, for pennies, to a local used rubber factory.

One day, my father, Abraham, heard through the grapevine that he could find a bonanza of old, free rubber overshoes up near a defunct timber camp in the Lac St.-Jean region. Getting to the timber camp was an arduous task and so my father decided to take his brother-in-law Sam Wiloshen with him as a helper.

They had to walk five miles to a rickety, old, swaying trestle bridge and then cross over the bridge and still go another few miles to the camp. The trestle bridge swayed dangerously over a steep ravine and rushing river. Each of them had a large gunnysack, which they were looking forward to filling to capacity with rubber galoshes. When they got to the middle of the bridge Sam tapped my father on his shoulder and said, "Avramel, stop a minute, my head is swimming, I think I'm going to fall in the water."

But my father thought to himself, "I'm young and I'm strong," so he told Sam to jump on his back and he would carry him across, and he did. When they got to the camp there were so many rubber overshoes strewn about it was a "Used Rubber Garden of Eden." Each of them filled their sack so full they could hardly walk. They started back over the trestle bridge. When they got almost to the middle of the bridge Sam again tapped my father on the shoulder. "Avramel," he said, "I feel dizzy, only more than before. My head is turning around so fast, I think I might fall into the water."

My father thought to himself, "I'm young and I'm strong," and so he told Sam to hop on his back and he gave him the two full sacks of rubber overshoes to hold. Just as soon as he took a few steps Sam felt so scared that he threw his arms around my father's neck and in the process totally forgot about the two bags of galoshes and both sacks fell straight into the river! My father was so mad he almost threw Sam into the river with them. My father never forgot how he lost his bonanza of free used galoshes. In fact it was one of the last stories he told on his deathbed. I've told it on tape, which has been sent to everyone in my family, and my niece, June Gould, retold it here, adding some of her words.

EDWARD DUKE, *retired photographer*

THE VACUUM

During the 1930s, all the floors in Noona's apartment at 300 East 152nd Street in the Bronx were linoleum. She cleaned them like she cleaned everything else in her home, including her two children. She used Fuller Brush scrub brushes, mops, and elbow grease. So when my father got one of his earliest jobs as an Electrolux salesman, he was convinced that his mother would love this new, easier way to clean.

The way he tells it, he gave his own mother the full sales pitch. He demonstrated how powerful the suction was even after putting a tissue over the nozzle. He showed her how the long, thin attachment got dirt out from between the couch cushions. He showed her how she could finally reach the ceilings. You should know that Noona was all of five feet tall, if she was that. At any rate, my father convinced his own mother to spend $69 of post-Depression money on her first vacuum. After all, what mother could resist, and what did it matter if she couldn't afford it!

However, a month or two later when he saw her take out her usual Fuller Brush broom, he realized that she had never used the new machine. As he says, "Little did I know, she was afraid of it!"

Years and years passed. My father and grandfather were the only ones to ever use THE VACUUM, until the grandchildren started arriving. Dad still did most of the vacuuming, but all five of us helped out. As we got older and busier, the next child in line took over. It wasn't until Margaret, fourth in line, that we found the ending for this story.

By that time THE VACUUM was almost thirty years old. It seems that one day Margaret decided that all she needed to do to get everyone out of this vacuuming detail was to teach Noona how to use her vacuum so that she wouldn't be afraid of it. It was at this point that Noona finally confessed, "Maggery, I'm not afraid of the vacuum, really, but if I tell Papa, he won't come and do it anymore."

VIRGINIA PERRECA, *writer*

GRANDMOM YETTA GOES TO WORK

Grandmom always told the story the same way. She was the eldest daughter in a family of nine children, Polish immigrants who had come to Canada when she was four. Her father supported the family by working as a ragpicker. She was allowed to go to the fourth grade in school, where she was an excellent student. She was happy there and took pride in her beautiful handwriting.

Her father took her out of school when she was eleven to help support the family. She always resented the fact that she had to work so hard, while her younger brother Al, "That lazy bum!" was allowed to lounge around the house in his dressing gown. Her father had her papers forged, making her out to be twelve years old, so that she could legally go to work.

She went to work in a dress factory. When the foreman asked her if she could sew pockets, she lied and said yes. When the foreman left, she began to cry. A kind, red-haired man ("I will never forget his face!") showed her how to sew pockets.

She became an excellent seamstress and quickly advanced to the position of sample maker, someone who makes up the samples so that the manufacturer can find out the most efficient method of sewing a dress.

As good as she was, she was not happy at the factory. She spent her time off at the movies, and copied the stars' dresses. I have a small photo of her in an ankle-length suit, wearing a broad-brimmed hat trimmed with ostrich plumes. She wanted to go on the stage. What happened to her theatrical dream is another story.

LESLIE MILLS

In your Process Journal, record your feelings about your family story. Answer these three questions: What does your family story say about your family? Was it easy or hard to write it? Do you think you captured the voice of the person who originally told it?

Samples

There may be several meanings to my father's story. To me it's my father's humor in the face of adversity, that we are survivors; to others it may mean that my father learned to accept defeat as part of life.

EDWARD DUKE

I think it shows my grandmother's sense of humor. Margaret says they laughed a long time over how she had gotten all her vacuuming done for thirty years. It really shows how gently she ruled the family. And rule, she did! But she always made you think you were making the decisions. There's even a postscript to this story. She eventually, and thoughtfully, bought a brand-new Electrolux for her family to use! I now have that vacuum at Myrtle Beach, and laugh every time I use it.

I found it hard to write this. I learned that I usually tell my grandmother's stories, but haven't taken the time to write them. My grandmother actually spoke with a thick Italian accent, which I have not been able to capture in this piece.

VIRGINIA PERRECA

I think it says that my father's side of the family were very competent but they had many unfulfilled dreams. Many members of this generation in my family are still trying to fulfill the thwarted dreams of the past generation. This story is very bare, the way she told it. Her voice is missing though. I'm not sure I can capture her voice.

LESLIE MILLS

PORTRAITS

[Portraits] are often as much a device for self-discovery as for discovery of another, because they reveal as much about the writer as about the person described. From writing a portrait you learn what qualities you notice and what you value in others.

—TRISTINE RAINER

Portraits are descriptions of a person. Portraits based on childhood memories can become the foundation for articles, novels, plays, short stories, and historical, sociological, and psychological studies.

Portrait 1: A Peripheral Childhood Figure

Reread your Memory List 5, "People, Places, and Things." Choose a person from this list who was not central to your childhood to describe in the left-hand column of your notebook.

As you write, imagine that you are taking a photograph of

the person. Get close up, then back up to give the reader a long shot as well; take verbal photographs from many angles. Try to include in your portrait what this person meant to you.

Sample

GRANDPA'S SECRETS (excerpt)

Out on that white stuccoed stoop in the Throgs Neck section of the Bronx, Grandpa Buckley supervised the ebb and flow of Sampson Avenue. His white hair and alcohol-reddened cheeks could have reminded people of Santa Claus, if he had ever decided to smile. He sat on the edge of that porch, pipe in hand, and would wave to neighbors as they passed the hedges. He always seemed friendlier to them than to most of his six or seven grandchildren, who were back and forth hundreds of times each day. My cousins said, and still do, that he never spoke to them. But to me, he spoke.

Several times a day as I passed, he'd call me over to offer his weather forecasts, or to give advice about good places to hide, or to ask me to get him some matches so he could light his pipe. He knew I loved the woody, sweet smell of the tobacco he used, and would let me sniff his tobacco pouch.

His weather forecasts usually accompanied his pipe-lighting ritual. I'd watch him aim his shaky hand at the pouch and wonder why he didn't miss. He'd pack that pipe with what the family called his broad Buckley thumb while telling me his weather secrets.

I remember the day he taught me "Red sky at night, sailors delight. Red sky in morn, sailors take warn." The sunset where the end of Sampson Avenue crossed Tremont, we could see clearly from the porch at 2928. The evening Grandpa showed me, oranges and reds were so bright they tinged his white hair pink. Until that day I never knew sunrises had any color, and told him so. As the first puffs of smoke dribbled out of the corner of his mouth, Grandpa made a date with me to meet on the front stoop every morning until I saw the "red sky in morn."

For the next few days I got up in the dark and walked next door to find him already silhouetted against the gray sky. It was still so dark that I could see the glow of his pipe bowl when he sucked in. I enjoyed sitting quietly with him on those mornings. He smelled only of tobacco at that time of day. Later on, the smell of beer made it harder to talk to him.

VIRGINIA PERRECA

Portrait 2: Someone Who Helped Your Family

Write a portrait of a housekeeper, elevator operator, doorman, window washer, policeman, doctor, grocer, butcher, stranger— anyone who may have helped your family—in the left-hand column of your notebook.

Samples

DOREEN, MY SCOTTISH NANNY

Doreen, my Scottish nanny, wore a nurse's uniform for no apparent reason. She wasn't trained as one, but she liked the strictness. She liked rules. One of the worst rules to ever have been broken was the execution of Mary, Queen of Scots, at the hand, so she claimed, of the jealous, barren Elizabeth I. Doreen proved her gentility by getting knocked up by the gardener. He left her paralyzed from the waist down after she gave birth to their twins. She was nineteen years old and I never saw her again.

LESLIE ANICE BARNETT, *writer*

AZA

Aza, petite, graceful, brown-eyed and brown-skinned, wrapped in a sarong of vivid color and pattern firmly enough to emphasize her neatly rounded hips and to produce a walk both innocent and seductive. Her hair was glossy, smooth, and knotted tightly on the crown of her head. Great gold hoops dangled from her ears. My mother's coral lipstick gave Aza's lips a shining Brigitte Bardot pout, and the pink was a startling contrast to her glowing skin. She was sixteen years old, a Malayan girl, amah to my British plantation family in the early fifties.

JANE SIMONE, *educator*

In your Process Journal, explore the character in your portrait by pretending that you are the person you just wrote about. What would that person say about him- or herself, your family, you, sex, politics, and death?

Samples

DOREEN, MY SCOTTISH NANNY

The children are good. Clean and well behaved. But the Missus is a little lax with them. Don't pay much attention to the surroundings because I never have much time and I never have much money to spend, so I don't go out! But I take the children to see good Queen Mary. (They have the statues made of wax.) I show them poor Mary on her knees all because of the jealous Queen Elizabeth. And barren she was too. Not beautiful like Mary. Mary was both beautiful and good.

Leslie is my favorite. I remember the time I was in the den stoking the fire and she came running in from school. I said, "Les, I have something to tell you." My heart was beating and right away she blurts out, "I know, you're marrying and going away." Leslie scared the life out of me.

Well, my betrothed wants to have sex with me before we are engaged, but I wait and wait and I make him wait. After all, I come from a good family. But the truth is I was pregnant with twins when I married. And the bastard left me in the hospital after I had them. I couldn't move and he left me. I was nineteen years old and had to learn to walk, by myself, all over again.

I never pay attention to politics. I don't care for their talk. None of it is for me. I am in trouble fast, but I don't think none of them can help me so I don't think.

I feel like I've already died. I was so good, so good to those children, and that's where I met X. He was their gardener and that's where things went wrong. We never should have . . . well, we had to marry and then it was twins and he was gone and I lay in bed thinking I'd already died.

LESLIE ANICE BARNETT

AZA

Mem and Juan have four children. I am their amah. Mem's clothes are so pretty and she has powder for her face that will make *my* cheeks pale.

The children are not like my brothers and sisters. I go to the bungalow from my place behind the kitchens and watch the children for Mem. There are three girls and a boy. Two of the girls are twins. I can't tell them apart! They like to play in the pond in front of the bungalow. I have to tell them about centipedes and scorpions!

Jane is one of the twins. She talks more than her sister and asks a lot of questions. Her one front tooth is missing and she's skinny. She decides which games they play. She has a doll which makes tears and wets its nappy. She calls it Belinda.

I have a boyfriend, and will marry soon. My mother

has talked to me about husbands and their desires and what will happen when I marry. Sometimes I think of it and am frightened, but when I am close to my betrothed, my fears seem to fade.

There is talk in our village that the British will soon go. I don't know if it's good or bad. The Japanese were so bad for our country—the British are better. Who will take over if the British go? What will change? It scares me.

Death? I don't like to think of death. I saw so many dead people when I was a little child, in the war. I fear death, but I know it will come one day. But I can't imagine myself dying for a long, long time. I hope I'm as old and toothless as the oldest crone in the village and that when I die it will be in my sleep.

JANE SIMONE

Portrait 3: The Kid Who Was "Different"

In the left-hand column of your notebook, write about one of the wild kids, the naughty ones, the destructive outsiders, the nerds, or the oddballs that you remember from your childhood.

Sample

THE BOY IN SIXTH GRADE WHO DROWNED

A corpse, three days dead, soaked in the river, eyeless, puffed like a balloon doll so the buttons strain against the cloth. No lips, just puffiness, as though the water tried to prove skin's tensile strength.

ANN BEALE, *managing editor*, British Heritage

Writing in your Process Journal, explore the person in your portrait. Pretend that you are that person. What would that person say about him- or herself, your family, you, sex, politics, and death? Ann Beale answered these questions in the following reflection.

Sample

IMAGINING THAT I AM THE BOY IN SIXTH GRADE WHO DROWNED

I wanted to see if I could cross the river. See the other side without going over the bridges. I walked across the railroad bridges, climbed on the barges where they keep the tar for on the railroad tracks. I even hopped a slow-moving freight train. But the river is always the big thing.

You go out on it and it's all around you—everywhere, flowing and so on. When you see it from the sides it doesn't look the same. Just laid out on a straight line, kind of like a road.

I used to see the doc's kid, that long-legged girl with the pigtails, hanging around by the tracks and the banks of the river. She looked like she'd like to go out on the river too, but I didn't talk to her. She was just a dumb little kid, and I didn't need *her* spoiling my trip down the river.

There are these falls, down below the last railroad bridge. I thought it would be fun to slide down over them.

Maybe it would be fun to have that kid with the pigtails along. Feel her up, maybe, only she's too skinny. Nothing to feel, like a boy.

If the borough passes that ordinance my folks were talking about, I could get put in jail for what I been doing out here on the river. Man, I don't want to go to White Hill. Larry Wilkes's dad's a guard there, and he's *mean.*

I'm dead now. It's not much fun and I hate how I look. I guess it's okay though because it'll make all those others, like Cackie Bittner, who's telling the doc's kid about me, make them stay off the river.

I'd hate to think I died for nothing going down the river over the falls.

LETTERS

The only true voyage of discovery would be to behold the universe through the eyes of another.

—MARCEL PROUST

Letters that go beyond reporting the weather and other mundane subjects allow you to write emotionally and authentically. Not only can letters give you a means to communicate with friends, relatives, editors, and the government but they can be used as a basis for nonfiction, novels, or plays.

Letter 1: Letter from an Ancestor

In the left-hand column of your notebook, write a letter to yourself from an ancestor you knew in childhood who is dead now. Let the letter tell you something important about how to live your life in the present and future. Look for the gift of wisdom your ancestor can pass on to you. Here is my sample letter from an ancestor.

Sample

LETTER TO MYSELF FROM MY MATERNAL GRANDMOTHER, LEAH

Dear Ettala's Daughter,
I noticed lately that you've been thinking about me and what it must feel like to be dead these forty-eight years. I'm writing to tell you that my grave is in the best place it could be.

Remember the picture your uncle Eddie took of you tasting a piece of wheat in the graveyard where I was buried? That wheat is the answer. It's part of what I enjoyed on earth.

Every week I'd knead the bread. My dear husband, Abraham; my sons, David, Eddie, and Morris; my daughters, Sylvia and your mother, Ethel, could hardly wait to eat my delicious challah. I would feel happy that I had made it with my own two hands. As I felt and shaped the loaves, it grew as smooth as my babies' bodies. As my children grew older I worked the dough and remembered my children's sweet smell in the morning when they suckled at my breast.

In the evening of my life I could feel my children's bodies grow and rise like the bread I prepared for them.

My graveyard is the place where the bread comes from, the bread you must knead for yourself.

When the wheat waves golden in the sun it is like my breath upon your cheeks. And when it rains I am flooding you with my love. When the wheat is cut down, and harvested, and grains fly into the sky, think of me as having become part of a multitude of starting points for you, my grandchild.

You were my daughter Ethel's first and only child. The three of us are linked like the braids of the bread I wove for the Sabbath. Think of me often now, sleeping peacefully in the wheat field of your heart.

Your Grandmother, Leah Duke

You sing in my mind like wine. What you did not dare in your life you dare in mine.

—MARGE PIERCY

Read over your letter. In your Process Journal, reflect on what you got from your ancestor. Here is my Process Journal entry on my letter.

Sample

My grandmother died when I was two, but she must have given me physical and emotional love when I was a child because that love came through when I wrote the letter. I needed to hear from my grandmother so that I could benefit from her wisdom and proceed creatively and courageously with my future.

Letter 2: Correspondence with a Childhood Object

Turn to your Memory List 5, "People, Places, and Things." Choose an object from that list or another that you have remembered since you made the list. Imagine that the object can talk. Let the object speak to you about where it went, how it's feeling, what it meant to you. Finally, correspond with that object in the left-hand column of your notebook.

Sample

GRANDFATHER'S PENNIES (excerpt)

Dear Pennies,
Where are you? I've looked everywhere I can think of and I still can't find you. I was sure I'd put you in the bottom drawer of my desk and tucked you way in the back. Please turn up!

Love,
Judy

Dear Judy,
We were comfortable in the desk and we felt safe. Occasionally one of your sisters would look at us but they always left us alone. We don't know who took us or why and we don't know that you'll ever get this letter, but we miss you and we love you.

Love,
Pennies

Dear Pennies,

I looked again in the drawer. You still weren't there! I keep hoping that I'm wrong and you haven't really gone. I worry that I did something wrong and that's why you've disappeared. I love you so much. You're the only thing that I can touch in order to touch Grandpa. Mom and Daddy tell me how wonderful he was, and to me, you're that love.

Where are you? I haven't cried yet. I hope you're just misplaced.

Love,
Judy

Dear Judy,

We're so close to you, just down the block. Little Jimmie took us. He didn't know we're special. He thinks we're just money. We're so worried. Life isn't good for us anymore. We're sad to tell you that he also took your grandmother's crisp dollars and spent them on candy and comic books. We know now that it's only a matter of time before we too will be gone. We're scared. Hurry and find us.

Love,
Pennies

Dear Pennies,

Mother asked about you today. I pretended that I didn't realize you were gone. I don't know what made her ask. I hurt inside because I wanted you back and if I told Mom you were lost, she'd yell at me and I'd feel even worse.

Where are you? Are you close? Are you still together? Who has you? You can't mean as much to them as to me. How are Grandma's dollars?

Love,
Judy

Dear Pennies,

I'm beginning to accept that I'll never see you again. It hit me when Grandma died. I loved her so much and wanted to keep the dollars as a remembrance of her love for me. She never forgot a birthday even though she had so many grandchildren and not very much money. I know two dollars isn't much and that I have the memories of Gram to keep with me always, but not having them is still another loss. My only hope is that you are all still together and that you remember how much I loved you.

Love,
Judy

Dear Judy,
There are only a few of us left. This might be our last letter. It's been some time since the dollars were taken and spent. Sometimes Jimmie throws a crumpled wrapper into the shoe box and we know one of us was spent for it, but we can't warm up to it. We grieve the losses as they occur. There can't be more than sixty of us left. It's hard to tell because he moves us around and is careless with us and not all of us made it from one spot to the next. We did love you and all of us wish we were still in the peanut-butter jar and in your bottom desk drawer. Maybe somehow, some of us will find our way into your pocket.

Love,
Pennies

JUDY LUSTER, *teacher*

What do you see as the potential for your letter correspondence? Discuss this question in your Process Journal. Here is Judy Luster's discussion of her correspondence.

Sample

My colleagues in the elementary schools have read these letters to their students and they have gotten very positive feedback from them. I think my Pennies letters have the potential to become a children's story. I can even envision the illustrations.

Letter 3: An Unfinished-Business Letter

Choose a person from your Memory List 5, "People, Places, and Things," or think of someone with whom you have some unfinished business. Picture things this person has done that still bother you. In the left-hand column of your notebook, write a letter to the person and tell him or her how you feel. Try to sound natural, the way you would speak if you were having a conversation with the person.

Sample (excerpt)

Dear Grandma,
The last time I saw you, Grandma, you were crying because you wanted to come home with me and see the house and the dog. "This place is awful," you said. You were afraid that if you fell asleep the woman in the next bed would steal your TV. You picked on this woman and called her Minnie Mouse because she had big black eyes, whiskers on her chin, and two big bushes of hair, one on each side of her head. That was naughty of you. I tried to explain to you that she was one hundred and one years old and hardly able to lift your TV. "Look," I said, pointing to the letter of congratulations from the president hanging over her bed. I asked if you would get a letter like that when you turned one hundred. I'm not sure if you understood.

It's been so long since I've thought of you, Grandma, and even longer since I've come to visit. I'm sorry. I'm afraid. I wonder if the next time I see you you'll know me at all. I hope that when I walk in you'll smile and yell, "Surrre." Why did you always say my name that way? But, probably I will say hello and you will just babble with eyes glazed without recognition. Or, you will complain loudly about the nurse who feeds, clothes, and bathes you and not notice me.

Remember when I used to wash your hair till it was squeaky clean? Then we'd dry it and curl it with the curling iron. Sometimes I'd burn the tips of your ears by accident.

Remember how you'd always ask me about my boy-friends and I'd tell you that I didn't have one and didn't want one? I do have one now, his name is Kevin. You met him once but I don't think you remember. We are going to get married this spring. We were writing up a guest list just yesterday. Uncle Charlie, Aunt Molly, and the boys, everybody. Not too big, though. I'm sorry, Grandma, I didn't mean to, but I snapped at Mom when she put your name down on the list. It hurt us both very much. It's not that I don't want you there, but it might be hard for you and for Mommy, too. I hope you understand.

The more I write, the more I remember the things we did together. Remember shopping at Trumbull Shopping Mall? It's much bigger now. I remember how you loved using your Read's Department Store charge card. They call Read's something different now. Yes, I know, I don't like it either. But I could kick myself for being so unenthused sometimes when you asked for a ride downtown. How could I have known then, and how much I'd now love to be able to take you to Bradlees to buy lawn furniture and flower seeds. Then maybe for a tuna-salad sandwich on rye toast with tea at Briarwoods's. Would you mind if I presumed your forgiveness?

I know after many years of being self-sufficient that it was hard to become content with being taken care of by others. But finally you seem at peace. You're not biting and kicking anymore, and you haven't escaped in months. Again, forgive me for presuming your contentment. It makes things simpler. Though unfair and kind of cruel, it is some-how easier to know that you've given in to your surround-ings.

So instead of the ride in my car, I'll come and sit by

your bed and rub Oil of Olay on your hands. Gently as I can, I'll pull the stubby little hard, black whiskers from your chin. I remember how they annoyed you with their touch but evaded your tweezers because of your failing eyesight. So we'll talk about my wedding plans. You don't have to speak, you can just listen and maybe squeeze my hand if you can. One more time, Grandma, would you mind if I let myself believe that these things would make you happy? It would help a lot. Thanks. We will talk again soon, I promise.

SHERRI A. CAMP, *student*

What was the hardest thing about writing your piece? How would you explore your feelings further? Answer these questions in your Process Journal. Here are Sherri Camp's answers to these questions.

Sample

The hardest thing I had to do was allow myself to feel my sadness about my grandmother. I cried while I was writing the letter. But because I was writing about something real, the scenes that I recalled only needed to be written down. To quote Donald Murray in *Write to Learn*, "the words themselves lend some of their own energy to the writer. The writer is controlling words which he can't turn his back on without danger of being scratched or bitten." I couldn't ignore the words. Once recognized, I only had to write them down, they were there for me. . . .

Letter 4: A Letter Settling Up with Someone Who Bothered You

Try to remember a child who bullied, bothered, or challenged you when you were a child. In the left-hand column of your notebook, write a letter to that person in which you explain that his or her negative energy turned into something positive for you.

Sample

Dear Ed,

Do you remember the day you told me about crossing the dug-out room in Grandma's basement? You said I was too young and too much of a baby to ever be brave enough to do that.

You know at the time you were right. I was too young to have crossed it then. But did you know you also set up the perfect challenge? In the long run that one small challenge may be the spark which ignited me, the spark which fanned the flames of my independence.

Isn't it intriguing to think that the person who you don't care for became what she is because of your words?

I really want to thank you. When I crossed that room I knew I could do anything.

VIRGINIA PERRECA

A lead line can be a question. How did you start your letter? Write some lead lines for your letter in the form of questions in your Process Journal.

DIALOGUES

> I do know that unless we care deeply about the people on our pages, we cannot expect the reader to enter into our stories. Once having looked honestly into ourselves, we should be able to look outward with compassion toward all human beings.
>
> —PEGGY SIMSON CURRY

Plays, stories, and novels all make use of dialogue. You can write dialogue for childhood dreams, for parts of your personality or your body, for childhood images, or for animals. Novelists, poets, and short-story writers use this technique to develop their characters. Writing dialogue will help you to gain insight into yourself and the person, event, place, or object about which you are writing.

In the left-hand column of your notebook, write a dialogue between yourself and someone from your childhood. Go back and forth, but come to some resolution at the end of your conversation.

Sample

DIALOGUE WITH MY ANCESTRAL GRANDMOTHER, EDITH BURR FLATTERY

PHYLLIS: Were you, are you, "No-Eyes," the old Indian medicine woman that I loved so much in the book *Spirit Song*? I thought about you as I was reading that book, and I came to believe— at least I wanted to believe—that you were my Indian guide and teacher.

GRAM: I waz yur granmuther Philly dear and I just waz and I did teech you how to plant in the urth and to gro parsley everywer and in the flower gardent to and rite by the stairz goin up to the swing and you could pick some and et it each time you came and it waz good for you.

PHYLLIS: But were you, are you, "No-Eyes"? She taught Mary Summer Rain to see, to see deep into her soul, to take herself seriously and to attain her purpose in life.

GRAM: Well Philly dear I don't no bout that but I did teech you to put picturz on your stakes in the flowr garden and they were more for a girl than just wurdz and labelz and we made a smudge pot to keep bugz away while we wurkt and we made a little fort on the hill out of the old lean-to the sheep use to have and I kept Bunker Hill, your first communion rabit from your Uncle Bill and we had many bunnies after that.

PHYLLIS: Yes, Gram, we did plant the earth and make smudge pots and plant parsley and all those made the bugs go away. Did you teach me to meditate or to see into the future?

GRAM: Philly dear, we uze to lie down together and take naps and watch spiders walk across the ceiling and you were afraid they'd spin down and land on you and we built giant bonfires and sat aroun and told stories and dreamed and most of all we planted potatoes for the winter.

PHYLLIS: Certainly planting food for the next winter was seeing into the future. Did you teach me anything about the spirit?

GRAM: Well Philly dear, I don't know anything bout the spirit but we did walk in the woodz and find wild flowrz and new springs when the old one by the camp dried up and you came to find me when no one was home when you were only five even though you were scared that wildcats might eat you every step of the way and Gram's house waz rite at the edge of the woodz and do you remember when you lost your little boyfriend Ronny and I told you that there were bettr fish in the sea that have never been caught and I don't know about the spirit.

PHYLLIS: Oh, Gram, you are you, and you taught me so many things, and I loved you so well.

PHYLLIS AMYOT, *sex therapist*

Why did you choose that person to have a dialogue with? Answer this question in your Process Journal. Here is Phyllis Amyot's explanation of why she chose to have a dialogue with her grandmother.

Sample

My grandmother was born in Germany, wrote phonetically, and never used punctuation except at the very end of a note or letter. She was definitely a woman of wisdom and nature, and as I was reading the book *Spirit Song*, I felt that the old Indian woman in the book was somehow very familiar to me. As I progressed through the book, I began to see that her nature was very similar to my grandmother Flattery's. I have wanted a guide and teacher for a long time, and after writing this dialogue I realized that my grandmother had been a wonderful teacher. Writing this dialogue allowed me access to the knowledge that I already had inside of me but had not seen.

POEMS

Family history is like a kaleidoscope in that you can keep shifting the
essential elements and coming up with new patterns and combinations,
but it is never ending.

—WILLIAM MAXWELL

Poetry is different from prose in that it highlights an intense
feeling or a moment of acute perception. It is usually lyric,
rhythmic, metaphoric, and abounding in images. Writing poetry
about your childhood can help you sort through ambivalent feelings, intense emotions, and confusing or paradoxical events.
Ordering your thoughts through poetry will help you concentrate
fully on one aspect of your childhood. It can help you see your
childhood memories through the sharpest of lenses.

The prewriting exercises of brainstorming, mapping, and
freewriting are very important to perform before writing a poem.
These exercises help you get to some of your childhood thoughts,
images, and fantasies that have been buried and that need to be
dug up before you think about creating a poem. Once you have
prewritten, you will be ready to put words, with unusual associations, on paper in the shape of a poem.

Poem 1: An Unfinished-Business Poem

Read this poem by Erica Jong:

MOTHER

Ash falls on the roof
of my house.

I have cursed you enough
in the lines of my poems
& between them,
in the silences which fall

like ash-flakes
on the watertank
from a smog-bound sky.

I have cursed you
because I remember
the smell of Joy
on a sealskin coat
& and because I feel
more abandoned than a baby seal
on an ice floe red
with its mother's blood.

I have cursed you as I walked & prayed
on a concrete terrace
high above the street
because whatever I pulled down
with my bruised hand
from the bruising sky,
whatever lovely plum
came to my mouth
you envied
& spat out.

Because you saw me in your image,
because you favored me,
you punished me.

It was only a form of you
my poems were seeking
Neither of us knew.

For years we lived together
in a single skin.

We shared fur coats.
We hated each other
as the soul hates the body
for being weak,
as the mind hates the stomach

for needing food,
as one lover hates the other.

I kicked
in the pouch of your theories
like a baby kangaroo. I believed you
on Marx, on Darwin,
on Tolstoy & Shaw.
I said I loved Pushkin
(you loved him).

I vowed Monet
was better than Bosch.

Who cared?

I would have said nonsense
to please you
& frequently did.

This took the form,
of course,
of fighting you.

We fought so gorgeously!

We fought like one boxer
& his punching bag.
We fought like mismatched twins.
We fought like the secret sharer
& his shade.

Now we're apart
Time doesn't heal
the baby to the womb.
Separateness is real
& keeps on growing.

One by one the mothers
drop away,
the lovers leave,
the babies outgrow clothes.

Some get insomnia—
the poet's disease—
& sit up nights
nursing
at the nipples
of their pens.

I have made hot milk
& kissed you where you are.
I have cursed my curses.
I have cleared the air.
& now I sit here writing,
breathing you.

Now, in the left-hand column of your notebook, write a poem about unfinished business you have with someone from your childhood. If you have written an unfinished-business letter, you may take some of the images and feelings from it and use them in your poem.

First, prewrite all the things that person said and did to you that you did not like and that still bother you. Let yourself feel how you felt when that person said and did those things. As you write the poem, let your emotions dictate the rhythm that you hang the words on. While writing, ask yourself, Am I being completely honest? Have I said everything I want to say?

Samples

SNOW WHITE AND HER SECOND DAUGHTER
(excerpt)

FOR JESSIE REDFOX

Snow White, rose copper cheeks coal black hair
I knew Disney on day one.
My mother, the Snow White I could not be

My mother, the Snow White I could not be
My grandmother's favorite daughter
You outshone everyone in her eyes
You eclipsed me with long red
nails, hair higher black than spit polished boots
or the shine on your kitchen floor

The messages for the day: "pick your
clothes up, the maid is coming to
clean
Your room is a mess
Men don't like dirty women, why
aren't you like me?"

You swished by,
a goodnight be good hung in the air
after your Loretta Young exit back then
when you played Snow White to my
ugly-duckling-never-swan-she'll-be.

                          JO ANN MORRIS-SCOTT, *writer*

PINKY

FOR GRACE PETERS CONNOR

You're framed in brown velvet
recessed behind dark wood in my dining room
You've been moved from the Plexiglas frame
with dried flowers that filled my
work space in a loft where
citysounds raced through the rooms

We've talked over the years
though your sudden absence
ripped open my suburban padded world
(Death is a reality—I'd never been

allowed to go to a funeral)
So I wasn't prepared to see you
quiet, thin lips unsmiling, no Pall Malls
no laughter
I understood then what it meant
to capture memories

But we've talked over the years
in the quiet of candlelit chapels
where I waited to hear your soft melodic voice
(I had to believe you heard me then and now)

I've always believed your spirit to be restless
traveling in limbo constantly searching
because the specter of death engaged you in his dance
When you didn't even know there was a party
Your bags packed with Christmas gifts
you'd finally given in to my requests
to come live in NY with me
and watch me become a woman

So I think your spirit is unsettled
even though I've shared moments with you
at the quaint pond in Vermont or
the seaside in the home of your unknown Haitian father
(only my shadow seen on the sand)

And even though we've talked, it's
your face with the sprinkling of nutmeg freckles
the smell of Chanel No. 5 mixed with cigarette smoke and
coffee I miss or the sound of taffeta and crinolines,
the feel of your black suede pumps, your long red
fingernails (I have my own now, a tribute to your
vanity) and pray those memories stay inside my head—
it keeps you alive for me
(I need a mommy to run to when I feel lost even now)

I've stopped blaming you for leaving
I know you didn't want to go
My anger has subsided
but I worry about your spirit—wonder if she knows
where she is and not in search of the railroad
to connect you to this side

I want your spirit to rest
Want you to know where you are
over there
not here on this side of light and life

I've shown you your granddaughter
whose long flat feet are yours
whose café au lait skin and thick brown hair
are the legacies you gave to her
She is fine and has your chair in her room
She said she needed to be close to you, too

We'll keep having our conversations
I need them
You probably do, too
Sit down and relax
Stop wandering
Know that I'm okay
You live for me in a different way

BRENDA CONNOR-BEY, *writer*

What was the process you went through to create your poem? Respond to this question in your Process Journal.

Samples

"Snow White and Her Second Daughter" was created from an implosion of feelings I experienced while listening to

June Gould read an Erica Jong poem written to her mother. Images sprang from my inner dust unclouded by the tears that separated me from them.

I began writing before June finished reading, intent on capturing the fragments of the images crowding in on each other. The process stimulated by listening to other poets was like a faucet falling off with the water turned on full. The poem spewed through the pen. Its mood and pace intact. The poem was nearly complete when I stopped writing. June's final process guidance, questions she wrote on the board—"Have you been completely honest?" "Have you said everything you need to say?" prompted me to look back again. I was surprised at how much would have gone unsaid had she ended the writing time without a final nudge.

The writing was effortless, natural, and seemingly automatic. The tension which usually accompanies any writing attempt was replaced with the awareness of the creative process and tension June initiated through the structure of her writing session design.

JO ANN MORRIS-SCOTT

The process led me to settle on my mother. She died when I was eighteen years old so she never knew me as an adult. I was raised by my paternal grandparents and was going to graduate in January 1963. I begged my mother to come to New York so that we could get an apartment together and then she'd be able to see me grow up and enter womanhood.

Christmas was fast approaching and my grandmother's house was filled with delicious spicy smells and I spent my evenings wrapping gifts for my family and watching the usual holiday run of TV movies: *The Bishop's Wife, The Bells of St. Mary's, The Song of Bernadette,* and, of course, *White Christmas.* But it didn't feel like it was going to be Christmas. I felt empty and mentioned this feeling to my grandmother, who also acknowledged that she, too, had a "strange" feeling. We never spoke about this again until Christmas Eve.

We were both reminded of our conversation when we received a phone call informing us that my mother had passed away—it was 12:20 A.M. and she had her bags packed to leave Philadelphia later that morning.

It's always been my feeling that it was hard for my mother's spirit to settle down on the other side. After all, she hadn't planned on a cerebral hemorrhage but she had promised me that she would come to live with me and she never made it. So, I've always believed she never had an actual sense of "closure." I've vented my anger at her for not living long enough to see me grow into the woman I've become—that part has been healed.

And even though I often go to churches and light candles for her where I hold my "mommy" one-sided conversations, and I've written several poems about her, I wanted to put my feelings on paper (to make my point a reality to her spirit as well as to myself).

I titled the poem "Pinky" because that was the nickname given to my mother when she was a teenager growing up in Philadelphia. I chose the free-verse poetic form because it's easier for me to think that way (sometimes). I think I'll play with the images some more and perhaps move some of the sections around so that I have a better flow.

All in all, I'm pretty pleased with the piece. I think "Pinky" will rest a lot easier now.

BRENDA CONNOR-BEY

Poem 2: A Poem Connecting You to an Ancestor

Look back at your ancestor letter. Based on it, how do you feel your ancestor transmitted his or her strengths to you either in your childhood or now? In the left-hand column of your notebook, write a poem describing the ancestor. At the end of the poem, see if you can connect something your ancestor did or was with what you were as a child or have become as an adult.

Samples

THE BIRD THAT FLAPS ITS WINGS

My grandmother Leah
made patchwork quilts
from torn curtains—
snatches of worn-out paisley shawls
tatters of lisle underwear and
frayed black satin snipped from
worn-out funeral frocks.

She wore high-button shoes,
stood in muddy country ruts,
stared at worn-out stones.
She wore long woolen skirts
even in summer.
Her hands held on tightly
to themselves.

My grandmother Leah
watched rickety wooden carts
pull cabbages and beets to market,
she touched her cameo brooch, rubbed
her hands with goldenrod to wipe
clean the smell of bread and salt,
scrubbed floors.
She sat on the red brick wall that
ran along the Black Sea.

My grandmother Leah
saw a blackbird perched on a maple branch.
Their eyes met.
She wanted to turn away,
to watch the boats, touch her brooch,

feel her coarse woolen skirt.
She wanted to turn away
but she couldn't.
She saw me, her unborn grandchild,
in the blackbird's eye.

Her future was in that moment,
perched silently in that tree,
alongside an ocean that is still
rising, beside a wall, along a peasant
street, among throngs of people coming
and going,
there, right there, see her.
It's my grandmother Leah.
She's walking swiftly back to her
small house
with the chickens and the cow.

She pulls a lilac branch from
the tree and smells it,
"this is my favorite flower," she thinks,
"this is my favorite flower,"
she will someday tell my mother,
"this is my favorite flower," my mother will tell me.

This is my grandmother Leah.
I tell you.
She gave me the lilacs
and the burning eye of the blackbird.
The hand that held itself moves this
pen.

See her wings flapping wildly
here right now, on this page.

                                        JUNE GOULD

CECELIA

I run my fingers through my hair
back on one side
then on the other
an unconscious gesture
until I remember
how I would watch her
raising her arm
slowly . . . with effort
placing her fingers alongside her head
then brushing them through the waves in her hair.

My hands are like hers
not in their deformity
but like hers in family
bloodline . . . in kinship.
They called her a cripple but she was a woman
with the heart and mind of a child.
She was willful and spoiled
she was quick . . . she was bright
and could walk if there was someone to take
hold of her arm or if she held on to the edge of the long
oak table
as she shuffled her feet to the other side.

Most of the time though
she sat by the window
perched on the faded wine velvet cushion
while she waited for life to come passing
by.

                                    MAGGIE MARTIN, *poet*

In your Process Journal, describe your experience of writing
this poem. How much did you have to make up, how did you
make it up, what did you learn about yourself and your writing?

Throughout this chapter you have had a chance to draft your childhood memories into varying forms. I have encouraged you to play with your images, memories, and ideas. My main concern in this chapter has been for you to shape these sources.

Now it's time to consider the next stage of the writing process: revision. You will find the revision process tedious, confusing, and isolating unless you develop a sympathetic and compatible writing response group that you can rely on for constructive feedback. Chapter 6 will help you organize and sustain your own writing response group.

6

Building a Writing Response Group

*. . . I don't have the kind of fear of the
unknown I used to have when it comes to writing
words down or reacting to words. . . . It's
because I have engaged in feedback workshops
over the last few years: getting feedback, giving
feedback, hearing others give feedback different
from mine. . . .*

—PETER ELBOW

I belong to a writing response group because it is the single most
valuable writing tool I have. I use it to improve every stage of
my writing process. Hearing how different people feel about my
work gives me an array of responses to choose from to which I
can adapt. My group helps me learn to appeal to many individual
readers and to handle their contradictory responses. Ultimately
the process forces me to decide what I need to do with my piece
of writing for myself.

Most of us have only seen the revised and finished versions
of other writers' work. Although it is inspiring to read these
beautifully polished works, it is just as important for you to
experience the struggles that take place before a perfectly crafted
piece of writing is published.

To learn how to become a better potter, you have to watch
a potter select the clay; you must stand next to the potter as she
or he methodically wedges the clay and pounds out the bubbles.

You have to observe the potter rolling the clay into malleable balls and feel for yourself the warmth and smoothness of those spheres before a vase or bowl is wrested from them. You have to watch the clay fall and flop out of shape and watch the potter start again and again until the clay finally bends to his or her intention. You have to sit in the artist's studio before the exhibition and see the pile of misshapen vases to appreciate the accomplished perfection of the tall, elegant, perfectly balanced urn standing on the pedestal.

My writing response group and I have learned the craft of writing from one another. I have seen good writing grow out of their misshapen and forlorn drafts. In turn, they have taught me to see the potential in my writing. We see things in one another's drafts that we do not have the objectivity to see in our own.

Reading, writing, and responding to one another's writing in a writing response group is a creative and dynamic process. By developing a small writing community, you will help yourself find a topic, focus on the most important elements of that topic, decide what to keep or throw out, and discover the current meaning of your memories.

Writing response groups provide members with even more than this. Group members internalize one another's responses, so they develop the ability to anticipate the kinds of things a larger and more critical audience of publishers, editors, agents, and the public might say. Furthermore, the dynamic energy created through the reciprocal processes of reading and listening, writing and reading, reacting and absorbing makes group members feel and act like the "real" writers they are.

Your group will help you feel like a "real" writer in two ways: by acknowledging and celebrating your writing accomplishments and by believing in your potential, which they will nudge you toward fulfilling. This support and stimulus in turn open you to the subtle ways that "real" writers weave their magic.

HOW A WRITING RESPONSE GROUP FUNCTIONS

In a typical writing response group, three to five friends, relatives, or newfound writing colleagues come together at a regularly scheduled and mutually agreed upon time and place. All want to improve their writing, and they meet to give one another feedback at every stage of their writing process. They do not dread these group meetings the way they used to dread their high school English classes; rather, they eagerly anticipate getting together to develop their own styles, voices, and meanings. They go willingly because they know that the group knows their intents, their limitations, and their potentials. They know that the group is willing to learn as much from their failures as from their successes. They don't feel intimidated by their group but rather nurtured, as Linnea Gugel, one of my students, does.

> I look forward to meeting with them. Their constructive criticism, ideas, genuine interest, and support are invaluable. In a narrative that I was writing about my mother-in-law's visit to my home they felt that I should have brought in more about the background of the situation and my true feelings.

SELECTION OF GROUP MEMBERS

You should choose the members of your writing response group carefully. It is more important for each member to be empathic, interested in you and your experiences, nonjudgmental, and willing to write than to be an expert at analyzing writing. Do not be afraid to ask writers more experienced than you into your group. If they are the right people, they will help you grow. If you choose people who never challenge what you have written, you may end up feeling like Kit Durney.

> My response group produced great frustration because everyone was being "so nice" that no one would give a truly

honest and helpful opinion, even when the writer asked for
it. All that the group would say was how wonderful the
piece was and "Don't change a thing!" Knowing that it was
a first draft which needed revision, that type of comment
was disappointing.

When seeking group members, look at the people around
you with new eyes. Is there anyone you work with who would
like to write about his or her childhood memories? Consider asking some of your colleagues to join your group. If you work at
home, perhaps some of your family members would be willing to
meet with you. In any case, look for people with a variety of life
experiences and backgrounds, varying writing abilities, and most
of all a willingness to remember, write, read, and respond. State
commissions for the arts and universities and colleges in your
area may be able to put you in touch with others like yourself.
   Once you have chosen your group, it may take time before
the members feel comfortable reading intimate selections to one
another, as Pat M. Rowan reports.

The first thoughts I put on paper were painful for me to
write, let alone read to my response group; yet from past
experiences, I knew that I must put myself through the
process so as to get at the writing beyond my tears. I per-
sisted. Reading to and then listening to Sherri, a member
of my group, gave me a little better sense of the direction
in which I should travel. She encouraged me to keep writing, saying, "You've got hold of something. I think you
don't yet know what it is." She was right.

Pat felt uncomfortable about reading for the first time; participants may also feel uncomfortable about responding honestly to
the work of someone they have just met. Time plays a significant
role in building the trust necessary for a group to be honest,
supportive, and productive. Here are comments by three members of a group that has met regularly for six years on how they
feel about giving and receiving feedback:

As time goes by, I feel I'm giving back something to the writers in my group. After all, they have given me the gift of their writing, and my response, in a way, is repayment for that gift. It encourages me in my own writing because it helps me to focus on what works and what doesn't. When their writing works, it sticks in my mind.

JUDY LUSTER

As I have become more comfortable with my group, the more open and honest I feel I can be. At first I thought the positive feedback was just creating safety—I was thinking about kindness to the writer. But I think we've all become better at what writing researcher Janet Emig calls "finding the emerald in the asphalt."

Also, now we're able to kid each other about what is bad writing. We'll just giggle about it, but that comfort took a long time. We've found that our group needs comic relief. We've been doing a lot of *written* responses to one another lately. It feels scarier as a responder because you have to be so much more focused in responding, but I think we might be helping each other more.

MARY WINSKY

If they are really listening, that feels good. Then I know that my opinion is respected. It's easier to see where someone else needs to revise, so in a way I'm learning about my own writing by being given a chance to help someone else. I used to worry about offending someone in my group, but the more I know the writer the more honest I can be. Rather than a shotgun blast, where I notice fifteen different things to comment on, I try to think about what the writer *wants* to know. If the people in my group tell me what they're looking for from me, then that helps me zero in on their problem. I give sincere, honest responses because I *want* the same from my group.

DONNA SKOLNICK

Judy, Mary, and Donna have learned valuable things from one another about how writing works, why a particular phrase or image evokes exactly the picture intended while another does not. They have also learned, as have members of other groups, how to stand up for their ideas and intentions.

YOUR RESPONSE GROUP

The capacity to sympathize or to identify with the experiences of others is a most precious human attribute.

—LOUISE ROSENBLATT

Imagine you are in your kitchen, living room, or office. Your writing response group has just arrived. You ask them to pull their chairs into a circle so that you can all hear and see one another, since body language communicates as much as spoken or written language.

At some meetings, each participant gets a chance to read and get feedback. Group members distribute copies of their writing to the others before they read it out loud. Sometimes everyone brings in something brief to read: a short poem, a line or two that has been troublesome, or a title for a vignette or story. Or they may simply need to brainstorm ideas for a new topic. They may have a mechanical question about punctuation. Sometimes members read many drafts of a single section of a piece, asking the group to respond to the effect of a single word or phrase. At other times members want general assistance—in selecting a good title or in choosing a genre in which to write. Often participants do not have a specific question but simply need reassurance that they are on the right track.

My response group gives me feedback on strengths but also on their confusion about my main points. That feedback is vital to centering my writing.

MARY ANN MATHEWS, *student*

At other times writers may not have anything that they want to read, or their writing may not seem to be as good as it had been. But in groups where the trust level is high, participants do not have to become discouraged.

> I can write something awful in my group, but my group knows enough about my history to let me take risks, to be patient with the times when my writing isn't going too well.
>
> DONNA SKOLNICK

Sometimes groups write together and then read their work aloud. At first they write about memories, but later they may write about anything that is on their minds. They get in-group writing ideas by looking through their Memory Inventories or by brainstorming new lists on topics that are of current concern, such as a parent's death or illness, a pregnancy, the loss of a job, a divorce, a personal illness, or the birth of a grandchild. The pieces that come out of these sessions are used either as warm-ups or as springboards to more elaborate writing; they can also be used to expand and enrich a draft that has already been started.

Sometimes a group member may bring in a longer piece, such as a chapter from a work of nonfiction or from a novel, a completed story, a long piece of freewriting, or several short pieces that do not seem either to stand alone or to fit together. At these times, everything cannot be heard in one meeting. Group members then have to decide who will read immediately and who will read during the next few sessions.

Sometimes it may be necessary to devote more time to one person than to another, especially if a member brings in a problem like the one this student describes:

> I brought two experimental pieces to my response group, one about masks and one about my grandchild Nicki. Pat, a member of my group, suggested they were really one piece, and that was so helpful. Nicki had just visited us and she was my "itch" and so in the end I wrote about her. Usually when things don't go as I wish, I find another mask is about

to fall off. I was upset that Nicki was not following the pattern of the family. She was bright, had been a valuable member of the debate team in her high school, had good grades, and seemed to me to be throwing away an opportunity. Struggling with that writing and having my response group support me in that struggle was an important step for me.

ETTA ENDAHL

If Etta's group had made a hard-and-fast rule about the number of pieces to be read in a session, she might not have been able to find the strength to struggle through an important writing and personal-growth experience. Furthermore, because she was given the gifts of time and support, she is now able to encourage others when they have similar problems.

Long-lasting writing response groups work extra hard to be sure that *all members get the time and attention they need* from one another. Here is what another student says about how much her group means to her as a writer:

My response group gives me the courage to go on and forces me to examine the meaning of my writing. My group shores me up, and increases my confidence as well as my knowledge. Sharing other people's journeys helps me define my own better. I enjoy listening to my group read as they revise and reorganize *their* drafts. They provide a model for me when I am engaged in the difficult task of revision and research.

PATRICIA R. FARLEY

Patricia gets a double benefit from her group: She gets direct attention to her writing as well as the experience of helping others work through their drafts. Her group members may bring writing in very rough form, or they may bring in a sophisticated revision. Whatever the form, the group focuses its attention on both the writer and the writing, asking and answering questions.

· · ·

Imagine that the group has agreed that you will read your work at a particular meeting. You find your place, get comfortable, and begin to read. As you read your work out loud, you keep a pencil in your hand—reading aloud heightens your ability to pick up errors. Put check marks next to the areas of your writing where you heard or saw glitches—tenses that did not match, a word that was left out, a redundancy, something that sounds confusing, and so on.

Look up every once in a while at the expressions on your group's faces. Are they smiling? Do they look bored, sad, or puzzled? Keep their expressions in mind—they are as important as, if not more important than, their words.

After you read, you must answer two questions. First, What do you think your piece is trying to say? You may not be able to answer this question immediately. But if you keep it in mind while you are writing and do not stray far from your original intention, staying on track will eventually get easier. After some time you will find yourself incorporating this question into the storehouse of questions you constantly ask yourself while you write.

The second question you must answer is, What parts do you like best and least? To build your self-reliance and inner direction as a writer, you must have a chance to say how you feel about your own piece before everyone else jumps in. One purpose of a writing response group is to help you develop the ability to evaluate and improve your own writing, not to make you dependent on other people's opinions. If you are clear about your own intentions and have been given a chance to articulate how you feel about your piece before you are swayed by group opinion, you will be free to play with *all* the ideas offered—including your own—and you will be better able to come up with an appropriate revision rather than completely capitulate to or reject your group's suggestions. Writing teacher Ken Macrorie says, "In the beginning the writer feels unsure. She should be encouraged. The group agrees to comment on parts or aspects of her initial free writings that they like. If they find none, they say nothing. . . . If they like anything—a word, phrase, ending, idea—

they speak up. . . . When enough free writing has been exam-
ined for everyone, or almost everyone, to hear praise from the
circle, the prohibition against negative comments may be
dropped."

    After you have answered these two questions, you will want
to know what the group thinks of your piece. Do they like it?
What should you change or add? How does it make them feel?
What sort of tone does it have? Were their senses stimulated by
anything in your piece? What part did they feel was unclear?
What did they think you were trying to say? Have you said it?
What else do they want to know? Do they think your piece
should be written in another genre? How did they like your title,
lead line, and ending? Ask your group some or all of these questions. Think of their answers as further data that you can begin
to sort through and utilize when you are alone working on your
next draft.

    In your group the members will join forces with you so that
you can see for yourself what should be saved, thrown away,
reshaped, or deleted. They do this by encouraging you to reflect
on your own piece through answering and asking questions.

    Your group should also use the following five exercises to
help you develop your own internal writing expertise:

1. *Mirroring.* Your group will tell you exactly what you have said
   and will try to say it back to you sequentially. This will help
   you hear what you have actually said and what you may have
   inadvertently left out.
2. *Entering.* Your group will pretend they wrote your piece. For
   example, if you have just written about learning how to swim
   by being thrown off a dock by your father, a member of
   your group might say, "When I was thrown off the dock,
   I felt enraged and terrified that someone who supposedly
   loved me would have endangered my life and my love that
   way." Entering helps you to hear and feel your group's
   reactions to your piece without being compelled to react as
   they do.

3. *Highlighting.* Your group will verbally highlight the parts of your writing that were outstanding by repeating back to you the images or phrases that they remember. Meaning resides in images, and highlighting reinforces image making.
4. *Relaying.* Your group will tell you the areas where they think you may be having trouble either focusing or finding meaning. This response will help you either to expand or to focus on aspects of your piece.
5. *Nutshelling.* Your group will tell you, in one sentence, what the piece means to them. This will give you more than one perspective on your piece's potential meaning.

While your group helps you to look at your piece through their questions and comments, listen to their varying perspectives and take them all in. Do not argue the points that your group makes; be as receptive as possible. Remember, you can delete, expand, or stand firm later, after you have reflected on their reactions. Your writing response group is a brainstorming session on the possible directions your writing can take. Reflect not just on the responses they give you but also on the answers you give them, for often these answers can be incorporated into further drafts.

During the entire question-and-answer session, keep your notebook handy so that you can jot down some of the questions or unclear passages raised by your group.

After your group has finished giving you feedback, take a moment to imagine that the deep scars caused by the sharp red pencil on your old writing papers have begun to heal. Then get ready to trade places with one of the members of your group and listen to his or her work.

GUIDELINES FOR WRITING RESPONSE GROUPS

Audiences can work for writers or utterly destroy them. . . . In my own composing, I frequently find that my writing is distorted or held back because I am trying to convince some professional in the field that I am knowledgeable about the subject.

—DONALD GRAVES

Establish a regular meeting date and time, such as every Monday at 7:30 P.M. or the first Monday of every month, and always meet on that date. Predictability will help you to plan and anticipate what needs to be done. Meeting regularly gives group members the impetus to keep writing.

Set up a rotational system for readers so that each member of your group can depend on being able to read and get responses over a period of time.

Begin each session with a meditation or a relaxation technique and a relevant writing quotation. Use either the quotations that appear in this book or other quotations from writers you admire. Your group needs to be familiar with other writers so it can go beyond its own notions; bring them in by quoting from their work. Hearing good writing helps you write better.

Write together as a group, so that there is always something fresh to start from. Thirty minutes is usually enough. These pieces can be springboards for long pieces that members continue at home, or they can simply be warm-ups for other writing. Even if someone does not bring any writing from home, there will always be writing to respond to if you leave time to write together.

Use this format for reading and responding:

- The writer *talks* about the draft.
- The group *listens* to and *reads* the draft.
- The group *responds* to the writer's comments and the draft.
- The writer *responds* to the group members' responses.

Vary your feedback by using written as well as oral responses. Written responses can spring out of oral responses, or they can be an alternative. I like to hand out blank index cards at the end of a feedback session. When the writer finishes reading, each of us answers the following questions on a card:

- What did you see? What stands out? What does not?
- What gift did you receive from the writer? What surprise?
- What was left out?
- What else did you want to know?

After they fill out the index cards, group members give the cards to the reader.

Recall out loud the visual imagery you remember from the work of the writers who read at the session. Say, "I can see . . ." and add the image you can see. If your group remembers an image in your writing, chances are it is powerfully written. This imagery feedback reinforces your ability to write powerfully. "Story Workshop" leader Betty Schiflett says, "Seeing is as natural to reading as it is to telling and writing; but most of us, in the process of 'getting educated,' have lost the knack of seeing what we read; we tend to read only for the retention of information."

End each session by discussing the group process—how the group feels about the format and the responses.

Review and evaluate the effectiveness of your group at the end of six months or a year by having a potluck meal together. You may want to discuss past meetings and plan for changes in time, format, or membership.

Ten Tips for Writing Response Group Members

1. *Branch out.* If you are always writing humorously or tragically, try to energize what Carl Jung called your "shadow side." Write in a mode or genre opposite to the one you usually choose.
2. *Accept your writing and yourself.* Don't get down on yourself if you do not produce "good writing" immediately. Give yourself what all writers need to become good—time, feedback, and practice.
3. *Focus on the important points.* Don't blast the reader or yourself. Focus on just a few important points that are illuminating.

4. *Value your opinions.* If you feel shy and reluctant to share your opinions of other people's writing, remember that the reader in your group is dying to hear what you think. Because there is only one of you, only you can tell that reader your perspective on what he or she has read.

5. *Respect your interior vision.* Close your eyes when you are listening to someone else's writing. Sometimes this helps you hear the piece better.

6. *Listen for meanings rather than mechanics.* You do not have to look at a writer's work in order to respond to it authentically. In fact, I recommend that you just listen without looking during the first reading.

7. *Become a writing response group troubleshooter.* Don't let the group deteriorate into a forum for arguments. Try to help members listen to feedback without being defensive.

8. *Comment meaningfully.* Try not to comment on the obvious. Speak only when you have something important to say.

9. *Write between meetings.* If you really want your writing to grow, you must work on it on your own.

10. *Be open and honest.* Inform the group of your particular feedback needs and let them know when they have or have not fulfilled them. Be honest, as you have asked group members to be honest with you.

COMPONENTS OF GOOD WRITING

After my students have met with their writing response groups four or five times, I ask them to compile a list of what they believe to be the components of good writing. Then, when they sit with their groups, they have a standard of reference. These lists contain aspects of writing to which listeners have responded positively. For example, some readers sense that they have written well when their writing summons smiles, laughter, tears, gasps, and/or a general focused attentiveness. They may feel they have missed their mark when they get little or no eye contact or see jiggling legs, tapping pencils, and bored looks. It is important for your group to develop its own standards of writing excellence, but while it does, you are welcome to use my students' definitions. Although there are exceptions to these definitions, it is best, as beginners, to be as simple and clear as possible. Later, as you develop, you can fabricate authenticity and introduce complexity. These definitions can also serve as a catalyst for your own brainstorming session about good writing. Here, then, is what my students and I think are the fourteen components of good writing.

1. Good writing *shows us images, scenes, and actions* and makes us understand what the writer believes.
2. It *respects our intelligence* and doesn't pander to us.
3. Good writing *flows*, carries us along and moves us forward to where the writer wants us to go.
4. It *uses active verbs* and avoids unnecessary adverbs, adjectives, and clichés.
5. Good writing *has a design*. This design may emerge unconsciously, but it is ultimately recognized by the writer and consciously carried through.
6. It *has clarity*; we do not have to strain to understand it.
7. Good writing *has a sense of humor*, which often enables readers to tolerate the intolerable.
8. It *is authentic and honest* and speaks from experience, or it is written so well that it sounds as if it is authentic—for example, Stephen Crane's *Red Badge of Courage*.
9. Good writing *surprises* the reader and the writer.
10. It *builds* and takes us by the hand as we climb together to the climax.
11. Good writing *demands engagement* from the reader.
12. It *is economical* and doesn't waste words.
13. Good writing *is mechanically correct*, but not at the expense of the preceding components.
14. It *can be complicated, obscure, and the opposite of everything on this list*, but only when it is written by either a genius or a seasoned professional.

Your writing response group can give you much more than writing feedback. It can become a forum in which you talk about your memories, longings, dreams, and decisions without the fears of being judged sentimental or neurotic. Try to construct this group not only with people who enjoy writing and talking about their childhood but also with friends and colleagues with whom you also have an emotional rapport. Once you have developed your writing response group, you will be able to get feedback at each stage of your writing process. How this feedback and your own critical faculties can help you revise and edit your drafts is the topic of Chapter 7.

7

Revising and Editing: Harnessing the Lightning

*The difference between the right word and the
nearly right word is the same as that between
lightning and the lightning bug.*

—MARK TWAIN

Revise means to see with new eyes. In revising a piece of writing
you refine, redesign, and rediscover the meaning of it. In editing,
the last stage of revising, you scour your writing for all language
and mechanical errors. A reviser's gaze constantly searches out the
angles and planes of a piece to see if it can be cast in a better light.
An editor's gaze is fixed on cleaning up what is already there.

    If you want other people to read your work, you will have
to craft it. Your writing response group will help set you in the
right direction, but you yourself must make the final decisions
about what to retain, extend, rearrange, and cut. To accomplish
this, you must slip out of your creator shoes and into the shoes
of a tough-minded critic.

In the four sections that follow, I will help you develop the tools
to make wise and creative revising decisions. The exercises will
help you

- concentrate on the content of your draft
- focus on its structure
- identify your draft's unifying patterns and theme
- edit your final draft

> One of the most demanding aspects of creative discipline is the revision
> process. . . . Such efforts require the same active intelligence as gener-
> ating novel ideas does. The process is like a dialogue between the artist
> and his or her product.
> —VERA JOHN-STEINER

You will need your notebook and pen or pens and your
drafts. Do one or more of your favorite meditations, and allow
ten minutes for each exercise.

CONCENTRATING ON CONTENT

When a writer finishes drafting, he or she looks over the work
and concentrates on the events, people, objects, and details
described. The writer asks, What is good enough to retain? What
needs expansion? And finally, Is this draft the best possible way
to take what is true in real life and transform it so that it gives
a better sense of the events than would a verbatim account? You
will internalize these content questions and answer them as you
become a better writer.

> The poem teaches us something while we make it . . . the poem requires
> all your capacities of thought, feeling, analysis and synthesis. I hope this
> might suggest that there is nothing dull about revision.
> —MARY SARTON

Whether your draft is short and sparse or bulky and cum-
bersome, sorting through its content will move it closer to its
elegant final form. Read over Patricia Farley's first draft, which
follows, so that you will be able to compare it with her later
revisions.

Sample

We would see Mother soon—this evening. We would visit her in Greenwich. We were in Wanamaker's where Daddy was buying me a pair of kid skin gloves and a dress for my mother. When he finished shopping he excitedly rushed us towards the elevator, pulling Dotty and me after him.

Abruptly, the elevator gate slid open—banging against the other frame.

Going Down! The operator called out in a loud and raspy voice.

Daddy reminded us to hurry as we had to catch the one fifteen back to Woodlawn. He pushed hard on the gleaming revolving door spinning us out onto the wet pavement.

"Damn it!" my father muttered under his breath. "It's pouring! You kids wait here for me!" My father handed my sister a large John Wanamaker dress box—a present for our mother.

Leaving us under the shelter of the building's awning, Daddy walked quickly towards the corner, pulling the collar of his overcoat up to meet the brim of his hat, trying to shield himself from the downpour. For a moment I lost sight of him, and felt the cruel winter's cold still present in the spring's rain.

When we got back to the apartment, Daddy made us grilled cheese sandwiches and dried our matted hair. My new gloves had gotten wet and slightly soiled, but I refused to remove them even while I ate my grilled cheese sandwich.

My mother had been away since Christmas—and I wanted to have her back, even if she couldn't talk to me. Daddy was silent as he cleared the dishes from the table. He continued to dry our hair with a large rough army towel. He desperately tried to comb the snarls and tangles from our hair as we whimpered in painful protest. Suddenly, to our relief, Daddy looked up at the kitchen clock. "A quarter past four!" He anxiously announced, "We better get going, kids!"

The afternoon trip to Connecticut was long and tire-some. Our progress was slowed by relentless intermittent downpours. I grew restless listening to the drum of the rain on the roof and the incessant swish of the windshield wipers. I fell asleep and was jarred awake by the screech of the old Dodge's brakes as my father pulled up to the entrance of the sanitarium. I could hear my heart drumming in my ears, keeping time with the pelting of the rain on the wind-shield.

As we neared the main hospital building my father pulled the car around to a side door. I watched his tall figure disappear as he entered the ominous gray stone building.

Finally we saw Daddy running back towards us with his head held down. He jumped in the car, slamming the door behind him, he threw the car into reverse, and he raced the old Dodge down the steep and slippery driveway. Skidding just inside the gate—he said nothing but tore out into the darkness of the main road straight into the heavy curtain of rain.

Suddenly, halting the car he pulled to the side of the road. My father turned to my frightened sister. "Dotty, your mother has had a relapse," he stammered. Then he got out of the car and stood motionless in the rain. I climbed up front and looked through the moving wipers at my father. He turned towards the car and got back in. Drenched to the bone he glanced at me. He had rain in his eyes. As he shifted the car into gear, I laid my head in the cradle of his arm. Feeling his tendons tighten, I listened to the blood throbbing through his veins.

That night I wore those rain stained gloves to bed with me.

Now pull out one of your own drafts. Follow the Content Checklist, making notes in the margins of your draft or in the right-hand columns of your notebook. Patricia's samples will demonstrate in depth how a childhood memory undergoes the revision process.

Revision 1: Content Checklist

1. *Controlling images.* The difference between an ordinary writer and a great one is in the quality of the language with which he or she bonds one image to another. Language without imagery is ordinary; imagery, however, invests language with the power to change the way your reader experiences the world.

> The controlling image is useful because it determines the language that informs the text. Once I know what the shape of the scar is, once I know that there are two patches of orange in that quilt, then I can move. Once I have the controlling image, which can also work as the metaphor—that is where the information lodges.
>
> —TONI MORRISON

Make a list in your Process Journal of the images in your draft. Read over your list. Is there one image that controls your piece more than any other?

Sample

> gloves, Dodge, rain, elevator,
> bars on my mother's windows,
> gray ominous sanitarium.
> The gloves dominate my mind. I
> want to make them more central
> to my story.

2. *Tone.* The tone of your piece is linked to your feelings, voice, and style. If you feel and see your experiences as you write them, your tone will have emerged naturally. Your tone reflects your feelings about the experiences you write about. If your first day of school was a disaster, for example, your writing about it might have a tight, anxious, frightened, or constricted tone. Conversely, if you loved going up in a hot-air balloon, your writing about it might have a smooth, light, bouncy, and weightless tone.

Long before the story is concluded, we, as listeners, react to the teller's
voice, to the overall resonance that emanates from qualities like the
teller's vocabulary, the rhythms of his sentences, his tone.

—BRUCE WEBER

Ask yourself how you felt when you first recalled the memory
that you wrote about in your draft. Did those feelings carry over
to the tone of your writing? Record in your Process Journal some
of the phrases that reflect the way you felt.

Sample

I felt elated to get the gloves, scared at being alone in
the car with my sister, and sad when my father said we
couldn't see my mother. I think some of my feelings carry
over, but not all. For example: "My new gloves had gotten
wet, but I refused to remove them even while I ate my
grilled cheese sandwich" sounds happy to me, but I don't
think I made my language fit how scared I felt waiting in
the car. The phrase that starts "I listened to the blood
throbbing through his veins" has a rhythm and tension
that reinforces my fear of being abandoned, but I don't know
if I got to the sadness that I felt when I realized how upset
he was.

3. *Objects.* The objects in a piece convey meaning, as images
    do. For example, the objects in an angry piece —such as
    scissors, knives, or broken glass—may have sharp edges.
    List the objects in your draft, and write in your Process
Journal about what they may mean in the context of your piece.

Sample

Gloves: they are smooth and tender, the way my father took
    care of us when my mother was away in a mental hospital.
The Old Dodge: it was protective and lumbering. It kept us

dry, the way my father kept us safe while my mother was ill.

The Ominous Sanitarium: this was where my mother was hospitalized for schizophrenia. It was cold and frightening, like her illness.

The Grilled Cheese Sandwich: it was warm and nurturing like my father.

4. *Symbols, similes, and metaphors.* A symbol can be an object, a gesture, an event, a person, a color, a sound, a texture—anything that reminds you of something else. A symbol expands language by substitution.

A symbol gains its power by repetition; metaphors and similes gain their power by comparing. A simile makes a comparison by using the word *like* or *as.* Both a metaphor and a simile appear in this verse from Olga Cabral's "Poem of Monday":

. . . far below in the narrow street
umbrellas butt their way
like ships in a rough crossing
chewed by the wind's teeth.

The comparison between umbrellas and ships is a simile; the ships' being "chewed by the wind's teeth" is a metaphor.

Make a list in your Process Journal of the symbols, similes, and metaphors in your draft.

Sample

Symbols: The *rain* is a symbol for the tears and sadness everyone in our family felt about my mother. The *gloves* are symbolic of my mother's hands that couldn't comfort me and also my father's hands, which did comfort me.

Metaphor: He had rain in his eyes is a metaphor for my father's sad feelings when he found out that my mother was still too sick to see us or to come home.

5. *People and their characteristics.* The people in your story are
   important not only because they played a significant role in
   your life but also because their attributes contribute to the
   overall design of your piece. This is the time to decide whether
   each of your characters is extraneous or necessary to your final
   draft.

   List in your Process Journal the characteristics of the people
in your draft. Describe how each of their attributes contributes
to your story.

Sample

My *father:* kind, considerate, agitated pulse, strong but upset
   on the inside
Me: waiting, looking at my gloves, tangled hair
My *sister:* she is younger than I am. I would like to show
   her reactions to our situation as a contrast to mine.
My *mother:* absent, not described, behind the gray building

The story will be about how my father took care of us and
about his love while my mother was in the hospital. I think
each of the other characters points up his qualities: my sister
and I point up his mothering and nurturing side, my mother
points up his disappointment and emotional side. I would
like to do more with my sister to show how she responded
to the situation. I have not done that yet.

6. *Audience.* Anticipating your reading audience's questions,
   concerns, and potential misunderstanding will help you focus
   on what it is you have said and on what you need to change
   or remove.

   Make a list in your Process Journal of the people who might
read your revised piece. What would they like to see in your
piece that you may have overlooked or deliberately ignored?

Sample

I am writing this story for me. It is the first time that I have been able to talk about my mother's absence. Maybe I'd like my sister to read it too. It might help her to see my father in a new light. My sister might want to see more about herself in the piece.

7. *Opposites.* When you include characters, images, and events that are opposites in your piece, you build up a creative tension that in turn helps highlight each unique characteristic. This tension pulls your readers into your piece and keeps them reading until the tension is resolved. Some classic opposites are Snow White and her wicked stepmother, and Othello and Desdemona. More modern opposites are Han Solo and Darth Vader in *Star Wars*, and Felix Ungar and Oscar Madison in *The Odd Couple*.

Have you developed opposites in your draft? If so, what are their contrasting characteristics? If not, what details could you add that would highlight opposite qualities? Answer these questions in your Process Journal.

Sample

What I already have in my piece:
My mother and father—she left us because of her illness/ he always stuck by us
The comfort and warmth of our home/the cold and gray sanitarium
My mother's absent hands/my father's hands drying our hair
The comfort and dryness of the Dodge/the rain outside

What I could add:
The isolation of the car/the business out in the world
My reaction to not seeing my mother/my sister's reaction

The city where my father bought my gloves/the suburbs where we lived

8. *Context*. Your memory took place in a world larger than your neighborhood or hometown. Many social and political events were taking place that indirectly or directly influenced your life or the lives of your parents. Widen the circle of your memory to include the events of the outside world. This will help you put your memory and your life into a more global perspective.

What was going on in your town or nation when your memory took place? How might that have affected your family life? Reflect on these contexts in your Process Journal.

Sample

We lived near a big city—New York. The pace and tempo was different than in the suburbs, where we were more isolated.

It was 1947, the war was over, and most people were buying new cars, but because of the expense of my mother's hospitalization we still had our old Dodge.

My father must have wanted to enjoy life after the restrictions of the war, but he couldn't because of my mother. Maybe that's why he splurged on the gloves for me—maybe he just wanted to feel like everyone else for a change.

9. *Genre*. Different genres have different rules. Think of the rules as maps that other writers have left behind to help you make your own writing journey rather than as rigid and un-yielding directions to be followed.

Jot down in your Process Journal notes to yourself about how you might have seen the main character or events in your draft if you had written your piece as a poem, short story, magazine article, autobiography, biography, or argumentative essay.

Samples

POEM(S)

> I would write a poem about my father:
> shaving as a young man
> brushing our hair
> standing in the rain

SHORT STORY

> I will write about the men on my father's side of the family.

MAGAZINE ARTICLE

> I might check with mental hospitals to find out the percentage of mothers who are schizophrenic and the effect those mothers have on their children.

BIOGRAPHY

> It would by interesting to write about my father like a men's column or a "Hers" column in *The New York Times*.

ARGUMENTATIVE ESSAY

> It would be interesting to write an argument in favor of being brought up by a father; and an argument for or against holding back emotion from children—which gave my father strength but kept us from knowing him.

10. *Voice.* Whoever speaks or tells the story in your piece has to establish a relationship with the reader. "Call me Ishmael," the well-known first sentence of Herman Melville's *Moby-Dick*, sets the stage for the novel. It is expressed through language as Ishmael uses it. The impression his voice makes on us clues us in to *his* opinions of his experiences at sea.

It is through your writing voice that you engage readers in your piece. Your writing voice inflects the words arranged on the page. Become more aware of the way your voice can undermine or reinforce the meaning of your piece.

Whose voice tells your story? How does that voice interact with the reader? Answer these questions in your Process Journal.

Sample

The voice in my piece sounds like me as a child. I think I was writing to myself in my child-voice in order to get back in touch with my father as he was when I was small.

I would like readers to enter my memory through my childlike perceptions—that is why I used so many sensory images—children retain images more than they do words.

Revision 2: Expanding Your Draft

Because of the way I was taught to write, I always thought of revision as deletion. It never occurred to me that revision could also mean adding extensively to already existing material. You may have inherited the same erroneous idea from your schooling and are now surprised that you are being asked to expand when your draft may already be huge.

In this revision, you should do two things. First, look back at your work and celebrate what you have already written that meets the ten criteria in the Content Checklist. Then expand your draft if any of these criteria have not been met.

Using your responses to the Content Checklist as a guide, write a separate draft. In it, incorporate insights about your piece from the checklist and add new, reader-oriented information. Then combine this draft with your original to make an expanded draft.

Sample

UNEDITED SECOND DRAFT: AN EXPANSION (excerpt)

My father bent down and slipped the tiny kid skin gloves over my hands, smoothing them out across the back and insides of my palms. They were small and fit my child's hands perfectly. They were smooth and white and smelled full of new animal life. A pair of kid gloves—only the rich kids could afford such an expensive and frivolous item. After all, what would a five-year-old want with such exquisite gloves? I would most likely lose them the first days wearing.

But Daddy didn't flinch as the sales clerk ran up the bill. Twelve dollars! In 1947, that was a small ransom. Oh, how I rejoiced in the feel and smell of this second skin!

We would see mother soon, this evening. We would visit her up in Greenwich. Daddy excitedly rushed Dotty and me towards the elevator.

Abruptly, the elevator gate slid open, banging against the other frame.

"Going down," the operator called out in a loud and raspy voice.

Daddy steered us in amongst the other passengers. As I stood in the suffocating confines of shoes and coat hems, I searched anxiously over the heads of the others for my father's face.

Suddenly the elevator's bottom seemed to drop out from under me. I frantically clutched at my father's pant legs, a cry of panic as my tiny knees buckled under me. But my father's firm grasp reassured and steadied me.

"Damn it," my father muttered under his breath. "It's

pouring. You kids wait here for me!" My father handed my sister the large dress box—a present for Mamma.

Leaving us under the shelter of the building's awning, Daddy walked quickly towards the corner pulling up the collar of his overcoat to meet the brim of his hat, trying to shield himself from the downpour. For a moment I lost sight of him and felt the cruel winter's cold still present in the spring's rain.

The lumbering old Checker cab pulled up to the curb. "Grand Central, please!" When we got there we raced down the stairs across the concourse, arriving just in time before the departure gate closed. We jumped into the last car. Out of breath and heaving with exhaustion, Daddy placed us on the scratchy mohair seats. Drenched in sweat and rain, he collapsed on the seat opposite us.

Our old 1936 Dodge coupe waited on the hill outside our apartment house. Daddy looked anxious as he started up the car. Setting the choke, throwing in the clutch, he put the car into gear. She bucked into first and second— finally making it to the safety of third.

The afternoon trip was long and tiresome. Our progress was slowed by relentless, intermittent downpours. I grew restless listening to the drum of the rain and the windshield wipers. I fell asleep and was jarred awake by the screech of the old Dodge's brakes as my father pulled up to the entrance of the sanitarium. I could hear my heart drumming in my ears, keeping time with the pelting of the rain on the windshield.

Once inside the main gate, we drove up a long dark road, through towering hemlocks, sentinels, laden down with their wet burden.

As we neared the main hospital building, my father pulled the car around to a side door. Parking the car under the shelter of a large fir tree he pointed up at a window.

"That's your mother's room, Patsy!" Surprised, I asked, "Why do all the windows have elevator gates on them?"

My father half-laughed at my remark. Patting my head with his large but gentle hand he never answered me.

Looking in the rearview mirror he removed his large fedora and combed and straightened his red-brown hair. His clear blue eyes and youthful face smiled back at me in the reflection. Replacing his hat, he reminded us to stay inside the car until his return. He stepped out into the rain, carrying the large dress box under his arm.

What did you add to your original draft? Why? Answer these questions in your Process Journal.

Sample

I added to the description of the gloves and the way my father put them on me. They were the *objects* that brought this whole memory back to me, and I want them to be more central to my piece.

I also added my memory of the department store and the whole section leading up to the trip to the sanitarium because I wanted to show the *opposite* emotions that my father experienced that day—his elation and expectation that my mother was getting better and his depression that she was in fact getting worse.

The other *opposites* I wanted to show were the strains on my father that day and his ability to still be tender toward us.

I continued with the rain because I think it is such a strong *symbol* of how we all felt—depressed, sad, relentlessly cold and grim. I added various new *objects*:

- the scratchy mohair seats on the train because they were a contrast to the smooth leather gloves.
- the Checker cab because it provides a context for my memory; New York versus the suburbs where we lived.
- the gates on my mother's window because they resonated with the gates on the elevator.

- my father's fedora because it placed him in time and because it symbolized his emotional age—he was old before his time because he had so many lonely responsibilities.

Although I am still writing this piece to express my long-buried feelings rather than to share them with a large *audience*, I am more willing to revise so that my response group will like it and empathize with me. I want this piece to be good because it is my memory and it's important to me.

The *tone* of the piece has changed. I added more moments—the elevator and the cab—where I felt anxious about being lost or separated from my father. Also the overall *tone* of this draft is anticipation, a rushed and excited momentum contrasted with my previous draft's slow and relentless waiting.

I think I created a *context* for my piece by adding New York, Wanamaker's, and Grand Central Station, while at the same time I provided a *contrast* of rhythms by taking the reader from the isolated and quiet suburbs to the more hectic and expectant city.

FOCUSING ON STRUCTURE

Your writing will become stronger if you articulate its emerging structure and consciously control where you want it to go. Planning how much structure you need to build into your piece before you write is analogous to planning a trip. Some travelers do not book anything until they get to their destination. Others—like me—book only major stopovers; we wait until we arrive before arranging for restaurant reservations, theater tickets, and walking tours. Still others like to travel with everything planned in advance—they often take package tours that include meals, museums, shops, and rest stops.

I plan my writing journeys the way I plan a trip. I decide beforehand where my major stops will be, but I leave myself the freedom to discover alternate routes, interesting byways, and further paths within the overall parameters of my story.

You need to decide where you fall on the structure continuum—and then plan and construct your pieces accordingly.

Revision 3: Experimenting with Sequence

We remember the events of our childhood in sequence. Things in adult life also appear to happen in a sequential chain. But the way we write about these events is not preordained to follow the same order. We can sharpen and reorganize our writing so that readers become enmeshed and surprised rather than bored by a predictable sequence.

Mapping out a time structure for your piece before, during, or after prewriting or drafting will help you reach your readers more efficiently. You can reorganize the sequence of your memory in the following four sequencing patterns:

- *The Clock.* A clock piece starts from the beginning of a chain of events and works through to the end of the chain. It can also start at the end and flash back, or it can start in the middle and move first forward or backward.
- *The Firecracker.* In a firecracker piece, one event causes another. Without the first, the rest probably wouldn't have happened.
- *The Dance.* A dance piece moves back and forth between various times or places.
- *The Analysis.* An analysis piece presents all the data, analyzes it, and comes up with a logical conclusion.

Map out the sequence you followed in your draft. In most cases, it will be the clock sequence.

Sample

My father takes us to *New York*.
He buys me *gloves*.
He buys my mother a *dress*.
We go down a crowded and frightening *elevator*.
We go to the *station* in a cab.
We go home on the *train*.
We take the Dodge to the *sanitarium* in Greenwich.
My sister and I wait in the *car* in the rain.
We drive *home* in the rain.
I sleep in the gloves at *home*.

Now go beyond the clock—which is the most typical childhood memory sequence—and experiment with the firecracker, the dance, and the analysis. How will your experiment affect your further drafts? Write about this in your Process Journal.

Sample

These sequences are intriguing. I don't want to use them in the draft I've been working on, but I would like to write some new pieces with these sequence possibilities in mind. I'm glad I had a chance to let my sequence evolve out of my feelings and story without imposing a sequence for this first attempt. Now that I have my writing legs, I would be willing to try alternative ways of presenting my material.

THE FIRECRACKER

THE DANCE

My father dies of asbestos poisoning from his job. He has been disinherited by his father, but he didn't complain.

My grandfather remarries and has another son.
My mother has been in and out of mental hospitals. My father never complains.

My father's father is about to strike him, but his mother—who is pregnant—intercedes. She is accidentally struck, falls against a wood-burning stove, hemorrhages, and dies.

Age 63

Age 40

Age 5

MY FATHER'S LIFE

Age 19

Age 15

My father marries my mother, who is nineteen. Both families are against the marriage. I am born.

My father is sent to a strict English-style prep school, where he is whipped. He *never* complains—while he is there or afterward—of his treatment.

THE ANALYSIS

Cause 1	Cause 2
My grandfather was brought up in strict English boarding schools. He held back things from everyone because he thought it was proper behavior. He was a stoic and proud of it.	My father held back things from us because he never complained and also because he didn't want to hurt us.

Result 1
I hold back things from myself to keep from feeling sad.

Revision 4: Exploring Leads and Endings

The opening of your piece holds the key to getting the readers' attention. If that key is chiseled and shaped properly, it will open the door to their interest.

Your lead not only has to hook the reader instantaneously

but also has to be so powerful that it sets up a chain reaction until everything—even your ending—is a logical outgrowth of its promise and intention. The beginning of your piece should foretell what will appear in the body of your work and in its ending. Sometimes a lead line and ending are the same, especially when the poem, article, or story comes full circle. William Zinsser says, "Knowing when to end an article is far more important than most writers realize. In fact, you should give as much thought to choosing your last sentence as you did to your first."

A lead or ending can be a question, a quotation, an anecdote, a statistic, an action, a piece of dialogue, or a declarative sentence. In your Process Journal, record the beginning and ending of your draft. What kind of lead and ending did you use? Are they compatible? Does one flow from the other?

Pulitzer Prize–winning writer Donald Murray says he writes "at least fifty or sixty leads for an article." Your entire piece will be improved if you spend time experimenting with various lead lines and endings.

Write some new leads and endings for your piece. Use the following definitions as a guideline:

- *Question.* If you ask a question as a lead, be sure that the answer develops as a surprise to the reader. Questions must be answered in the body of your piece; the ending can sum up the answers.
- *Quotation.* Beginning with a quotation can lend voice to a piece, but if it is not used skillfully a quotation can take your reader off track. You may also want to end with a quotation, wrapping up your piece.
- *Anecdote.* An anecdote is a brief story that presents, in microcosm, what will happen in the rest of the piece. Be careful with this one—it can sometimes be misleading. Relate the ending of your piece to the lead either by completing the anecdote that appeared at the beginning or by repeating it.
- *Statistic.* Statistics can lend authority to your piece but can also make it sound abstract, and they are less personal than

other leads. If you use statistics, the ending should echo or develop the statistics in your lead.

- *Action.* Leading with an action pulls your reader into the tension or momentum of the piece. Ending with an action leaves your reader feeling that the story is still alive after he or she has finished reading it.
- *Dialogue.* Dialogue lets the reader into two characters' minds immediately. The reader hears one character speak and another respond. This lead is very dramatic when used well. It is effective as an ending for the same reason.
- *Declarative sentence.* A declarative sentence will be told as a narrative. Professional writers often start this kind of lead with information gathered from the end of their piece to pull their readers in. A declarative sentence is also effective as an ending because it can unite the various elements in your piece.

Samples

Lead

Question
Why does the memory of a simple pair of kid gloves make me feel so sad?

Quotation
"You may be able to see your mother today, so hurry up, we have to go to New York to buy her a dress before we go up to Connecticut. Maybe she'll be able to wear it to church on Easter Sunday."

Anecdote
When I was five I fell in love with my kid gloves. I'm

Ending

Isn't it sad that the only hands that caressed my five-year-old face on that day were my own?

"She won't be home today and probably not for Easter either and all the days she won't be here I'll take care of you, don't worry."

As night fell on our family in 1947 I brought those

Anecdote(cont.)

not sure why, really. My father bought them for me in
1947.

gloves to bed with me, caressing my face like my
mother did when she was
well.

Statistic

Over 20,000 mothers are
hospitalized with schizophrenia every year.

More than 40,000 children
go to bed every night missing their mothers, who are
in mental hospitals.

Action

My father bent down and
slipped the tiny kid gloves
over my hands, smooth-
ing them out across the
backs and insides of my
palms.

Same as lead

Dialogue

"Don't wear those gloves in
the rain, you have to save
them for Easter."
"But they remind me of
Mother's hands, I want
to wear them all the
time."

"I will never take these
gloves off, Daddy. I want to
wear them all the time."
"I understand, darling, I
wish I had gloves like yours
to keep my hands warm."

Lead

Declarative sentence

It was raining.

Ending

The rain just never seemed
to stop in my life.

Decide what you will do with these new leads and endings. Record your decisions in your Process Journal.

IDENTIFYING UNIFYING PATTERNS AND THEMES

Patterns and themes recur in your writing without your being conscious of them. This section will help you recognize the underlying patterns and themes embedded in your writing, and it will show you how to follow them, to capitalize on them, to connect them to the whole of your work, and, in Eudora Welty's words, "to comb the thick tangle to see what precious strands remain."

1. *Patterns and themes.* As you look back at your draft, you may see a pattern or theme that pulls you like a magnet toward the important elements of your piece. Writers are constantly searching for those glimmering metallic threads that can pull all the elements of their piece together.

   What is the "magnet" in your piece that draws everything else together? Record it in your Process Journal.

Sample

I wrote the story to get to know my father better. He didn't tell us much so I had to go back to my childhood to get a glimpse of him again. I think he is the magnet that holds the piece together. He is in every scene, showing rather than telling about himself.

2. *Private words.* Be careful either to explain or to avoid private words. When I write "the lake," it triggers my childhood memories of Kirkland Lake, Ontario, where I picked blueberries, got stung by leeches, slept in a double bed with my friend Vivian Ironstone, and heard my mother and Vivian's mother, Toby, on the other side of the partition laughing and telling stories about their youth. But readers cannot experience my associations with "the lake" unless I give them details.

Write down the private words in your piece in your Process Journal. Have you fleshed them out with details?

Sample

My private words are rain, train, cab, Dodge, sanitarium, gloves, father. I have fleshed out some of these words but need to do more.

3. *Construction of meaning.* Whatever you write, conveying your meaning is your most important task. Writing will help you to think beyond what you already know and *create* meaning out of the infinite number of events touching your life. Think about the information in your piece, and constantly ask yourself why the piece is important. If you do not know or care about the meaning of your piece, neither will your readers.

Ask yourself, Why should readers care about my piece? and write down your reflections in your Process Journal.

Sample

It will help readers recognize the pain mental illness causes in families. It may help them come to terms with that in their own family. The meaning for me is that though my father was helpless in the face of my mother's illness, he was nurturing to my sister and me. Perhaps readers who have similar family problems will know that others have gone through this, too. They also might recognize that it is important to children to express feelings through language rather than hide them.

EDITING YOUR FINAL DRAFT

Fighting clutter is like fighting weeds. The writer is always slightly behind.
—WILLIAM ZINSSER

Read over your expanded draft and determine what can be cut. Writing should be as clutter-free and clear as possible. Cut and prune your piece so that it has room to breathe. As Zinsser says, "Use your shears and be merciless." The following eleven-point checklist will help you edit your piece.

Revision 5: Editing Checklist

1. Read your draft aloud. You will hear what is wrong as you listen to your piece; the problems will trip up your tongue. Your ears will confirm what sounded good in your mind, too.
2. Become your own critic. Say editorial things to yourself, such as Why did I put that in? Can't I say this in fewer words? What did I mean by that? or I don't get it.
3. Read to see if your draft is too long, too short, detailed, to the point.
4. Prune the scaffolding. Often your first two paragraphs are warm-ups and can be cut. Cover the first two paragraphs of your draft and see if you can do without them.
5. Play with your title. Is it catchy, and will it hook the reader? Many writers do not write their own titles, but it helps your overall content when the title is good. Write ten titles for your piece and choose the best.
6. Watch your verbs. Place them close to your subject. Make them active.
7. Get rid of unnecessary adverbs, complicated tenses, complicated words, and repetition. Delete sexist, ageist, or racist language and private words.
8. Be sure that each paragraph makes a complete point, that it sounds like you, and that it flows. Have you given your reader enough information?
9. Enrich your language with visual imagery. Avoid clichés and sentences and paragraphs that are not in sequence.
10. Vary your paragraphs so that shorter ones are used for clarification

11. Make each bit of information authentic, factual, and part of a context.

After you have proofread, and corrected any errors, you will have a final edited and revised draft. Compare Patricia Farley's final draft, which follows, with her first draft, at the beginning of this chapter.

Sample

KIDSKIN GLOVES

My father bent down and slipped the tiny kidskin gloves over my hands, smoothing them out across the backs and insides of my palms. They were smooth and white and smelled of new animal life.

A pair of kid gloves—only the rich kids could afford such an expensive and frivolous item. What would a five-year-old want with such exquisite gloves? I would probably lose them the first day I wore them, but Daddy didn't flinch as the salesclerk rang up the bill. Twelve dollars! In 1947 that was a small ransom. Oh, how I rejoiced in the feel and smell of this second skin!

We would see Mother soon, this evening. We would visit her up in Greenwich. Daddy rushed Dotty and me towards the elevator. Abruptly, the elevator gate slid open. "Going down," the operator announced in a raspy voice. Daddy steered us in amongst the other passengers. As I stood in the suffocating confines, I searched anxiously over the heads of the others for my father's face.

Suddenly the elevator's bottom seemed to drop out from under me. I frantically clutched at my father's legs, gulping back a cry of panic as my tiny knees buckled under me. My father's firm grasp reassured and steadied me.

As we left the store, Daddy reminded us to hurry, we had to catch the one fifteen back to Woodlawn. He pushed hard on the gleaming revolving door, spinning us out onto the wet pavement.

"It's pouring," my father said. "You kids wait here for me!" He handed my sister a large John Wanamaker's dress box. It had the dress he had bought for Mama in it. Leaving us under the store canopy, Daddy walked quickly towards the corner. He pulled up the collar of his overcoat to meet the brim of his hat. For a moment I lost sight of him and felt the cruel winter's cold still present in the spring's rain.

The lumbering old Checker cab pulled up to the curb. "Grand Central, please!" The meter ticked away as Daddy, Dotty, the dress box, and I sped to the station. When we got there we raced down the stairs, across the concourse, arriving just before the departure gate closed. We jumped into the last car. Out of breath and heaving with exhaustion, Daddy placed us on the scratchy mohair seats. Drenched with sweat and rain, he collapsed on the seat opposite us.

The rain let up as we reached home. Daddy made us lunch and dried our matted hair. My new gloves were wet and slightly soiled, but I wouldn't take them off, not even while I ate my grilled cheese sandwich. "Will Mama be coming home with us tonight, Daddy?" I asked. Daddy narrowed his eyes. He didn't answer immediately but gazed out the windows first. "No, Patsy, but the doctors promised that you could see her today."

We would see Mother soon, visit her up in Greenwich. She had been away since Christmas, and I wanted her back, even if she couldn't talk to me. Daddy was silent as he cleared the dishes from the table.

Our old 1936 Dodge coupe waited on the hill outside our apartment house. Daddy looked anxious as he started up the car. "I hope she'll make it to Greenwich!" Daddy said, turning towards my sister, who was sitting next to him in Mama's usual seat. I had retreated to the dark backseat. Sprawling out on its hard surface, I pressed my face against the cool, damp leather.

My father pulled the car around to the side of the ominous gray stone building. He pointed up at the window on the second floor. I asked Daddy, "Why do all the windows have elevator gates on them?" My father half-laughed and reminded us to stay in the car until he returned.

We waited in the old Dodge for what seemed like an eternity, drawing pictures in our breath on the windows, listening to the never-ending rain beating down on the old car. Daddy wanted to buy a new car when the war was over, but now, with Mama's nerves gone bad, he couldn't afford it. We watched as water gushed out the building's down-spouts, flooding the ground below.

Finally, Daddy ran back towards us with his head held down. Jumping in the car, he threw the gears into reverse, squealed into first as he raced the old Dodge down the steep and slippery driveway. Skidding just inside the gate, he said nothing but tore out into the darkness of the main road, straight into the heavy curtain of rain.

Suddenly, halting the car, he pulled to the side of the road. He turned to us and stammered, "Your mother has had a relapse." Then he got out of the car and stood motionless in the rain. Dotty quickly escaped to the refuge of the backseat. Placing her face against the upright, she tried to muffle her convulsive sobs. When Daddy got back in the car he had rain in his eyes. As he shifted gears I lay my head in the cradle of his arm, feeling his tendons tighten. I listened to the swish of his blood throbbing through his veins.

That night I wore those rain-stained kid gloves to bed, caressing their skins still fragrant with animal life.

Questions Students Commonly Ask About Revising:

How do I find the best starting place in the mass of words I seem to generate in my drafts?

Reread your work away from your regular writing place. Read it quickly to yourself several times. Listen for the place where you think it is possible to begin even if that place is your last paragraph. That paragraph has probably attracted you because it is charged by a quotation, anecdote, or statistic. Rework your piece using that paragraph or line as your lead.

How do I know what to cut in my piece and what to leave alone?

Select what you will keep and develop those points fully. Do a line-by-line reading, and nip anything that detracts from or repeats your main ideas. Be sure to read your piece aloud between each snip of the scissors.

How can I tell when my piece is good enough to stop revising?

When your sentences and paragraphs are varied in length, your verbs are all active, your language is simple and clear, your piece includes quotations, anecdotes, or statistics, and your story is fleshed out with sensory details.

Why do my freewrites and drafts sometimes sound more authentic than my revisions?

Revising and editing are human processes that grow out of your moods, emotions, and attitudes at a particular moment in your life. If your writing sounds stilted and dried out after a revision, investigate three possible factors: you are under personal or environmental stress; the subject matter bores or frightens you; you fear your audience. When you pinpoint the cause of your problem, you will be well on your way to managing it.

Is there a way to resequence a draft without rewriting the whole piece?

You can cut your writing apart and spread the segments out on a table or on the floor. Shift sentences and paragraphs around until you get a feel for what the piece might sound like rearranged. Writers call this cutting and pasting. Word-processing programs include cutting-and-pasting capabilities.

I try to make my writing sound clear but it still sounds convoluted and jumbled. How do I overcome this problem?

All writers—professional or not—have similar difficulties. The only cure is the desire and time to rewrite the section, one sentence at a time, until it relaxes and becomes lucid. Often after rewriting a recalcitrant paragraph ten or twenty times, I simply give up and put it aside for a day or two. My unconscious mind seems to work well while I sleep, exercise, or read a novel. When I come back to those tangled words, I can easily straighten them out.

I tend to underwrite. How do I cure this habit?

Jot down the questions your writing response group asks you. Answer them as you revise.

How do I know whether my piece will keep readers interested?

Listen to its rhythm and pace as you read it aloud to yourself and to your writing response group, friends, and colleagues. Check where your phrases might flow faster or slower and where you or your audience felt confused. Underline or circle the sections that you believe will fascinate readers.

Do you recommend handwritten or typewritten revisions?

Many writers still write their drafts in longhand, but many use word processors and say that they could never go back to typewriters or longhand again. The word processor is ideal for revising and editing because it allows you to add and delete while it stores your original drafts.

How do I know if my writing is good enough to send to a publisher?

If you and your writing response group think it is, and it has met the criteria for good writing, try it.

By now, the neglected writer in you has emerged, strong and creative, transformed by the power of your childhood memories at the service of your writing. Those same memories have the power to transform your life as a student, and that metamorphosis is the topic of Chapter 8.

8

From Memories to Ideas: A Student Metamorphosis

An enormous amount of other learning must take place before one can write worthwhile essays of ideas. . . . All writing teaches exposition.

—JAMES MOFFETT

We are all students, even if we are not actually enrolled in school. We are students of movies, literature, politics, TV, our children, our families, and our memories.

When you, as a student, break away from the banal, the mundane, and the obvious, those around you—including your teachers—will also be inspired. Here are a few points intended to help you sharpen your perception of the world as it presents itself to you.

PRACTICE YOUR WRITING

If you would be a reader, read; if a writer, write.

—EPICTETUS

Miss Hatton never let us practice writing, but my high school English teacher Miss Genung used to tell my class that we would improve as writers if we practiced writing every day. Every day! I was incredulous. What in the world would I write about—me, an ordinary person from boring Brooklyn? I didn't practice writing every day; in fact, the only time I wrote at all was for school assignments. I thought, in those years—and throughout high school, college, and graduate school—that professional writers must have spectacular experiences that trigger the stories they are meant to tell.

After I began writing about my memories, I realized that all my writing—essays, reports, letters, poetry, and note taking—had improved. Miss Genung had been right; the more I wrote, the better I became. Having spectacular experiences had nothing to do with my writing ability. My writing improved when I regularly practiced writing about my memories—ordinary as they were—and so will yours.

RESPECT YOUR IMAGINATION

In a photograph of myself taken when I was very young, I am sitting on a chair posed against a mirror. I look sleepy, and my pompadour and long, dark hair are messy. I am wearing a dress with puffed sleeves, and my eyes are puffy, too. I do not remember exactly when the picture was taken, but my mother tells me that the photographer—my uncle Eddie—was en route to his wartime assignment with the Canadian Air Force. He arrived at my parents' apartment in the middle of the night to say good-bye before being shipped off. Before he left, they awoke and dressed me, and Uncle Eddie took my picture.

Sometimes I think I can remember being awakened, and I imagine coming into the living room, rubbing the sleep out of my eyes and dutifully posing for my uncle. I think I feel afraid in that memory, afraid of the bare light bulbs, afraid of the stranger who wants to hold and kiss me and take my picture, afraid of the break in our routine. Although I do not remember the actual photographic event, I do recall that my uncle gave me a spare button from his uniform as a souvenir. I used to keep the bright brass button in a little dish next to my bed and hold it in my hand like a good-luck charm before falling asleep at night.

In my imagination I have reconstructed how I felt that night during the photography session, but this invented memory is as imprinted in my mind as the design of the brass button was imprinted on my hand. You have probably used your own imagination in the reconstruction of your childhood, too, and no one, perhaps not even you, can tell the difference between what you *actually* remember and what you *imagine* that you remember.

You can use your imagination to create poetry, stories, and novels as well. You can also use it to understand and analyze characters and incidents in literature, psychology, sociology, and history.

Start with what you know at the time when you are about to write. Then expand and embellish your statements, descriptions, and examples with your imagination, as I did with my middle-of-the-night photography session.

LET THE WRITING PROCESS IMPROVE ALL YOUR WRITING

In literature the autobiographical is transformed. It is no longer the writer's own experience: it becomes everyone's.

—STEPHEN SPENDER

All of the exercises you used to write your memories—prewriting, drafting, revising, and writing response group feedback—can also be used to develop essays, reports, and research projects. Before writing each chapter of this book, for example, I brainstormed its contents; mapped each section; freewrote most of the paragraphs; drafted, revised, and edited the manuscript; and got feedback from friends, family, colleagues, and my writing response group.

Leave plenty of time to craft your writing. Reports written a night or two before they are due are only freewrites or drafts at best. For one thing, you need time away from your draft to perceive it objectively when you read it again. For another, you need the feedback and support of your writing response group. When you allow yourself time to enjoy the process of writing as well as the product, your product will improve.

SHIFT FROM CHILDHOOD NARRATIVE TO EXPOSITORY WRITING

> It is memory that reaches tentacles out into each of these three different "times"—the time now, the time then, and the time of an individual's historic context.
>
> —JAMES OLNEY

I recently attended a high school reunion. I saw friends and acquaintances whom I had not seen in over thirty years. I wrote about my memories of them. These were rich memories, and I was glad to have them in my journal to look at and enjoy. But I could also have put them into the broader context of expository writing: an essay, a research paper, or a report.

To make the step from personal to expository writing, I would have had to look at my memories through a new lens, one that would help me perceive my memories' meaning in political, social, psychological, economic, or literary terms. I would also have had to discard the sequence of my memories, an order of events, and replace it with a sequence of ideas. In the process of shifting my lens, I would have come to perceive my memories not only as a statement about one life but as a springboard to statements about all lives.

Think of your memories as springboards to larger issues that might interest a sociologist, historian, psychologist, anthropologist, or biologist. Any one of your memories can become transformed into a research investigation. First, you need to think about your hunches in regard to your memories. Hunches are really hypotheses, and when validated they become theories. Here are some of the hunches my memories generated:

	Hunch
Playing in the Prospect Park playground	Having a playground created a sense of community among neighborhood residents.
Walking to school	Those of us who walked to school may have lower adult cholesterol than those who rode.
Being seated according to IQ in Miss Hatton's class	Telling children about their IQs stimulates bright children and undermines slower children.
Listening to the radio every night before I fell asleep	Adults who grew up in the 1940s and listened to the radio have better reading skills than TV-oriented children.
Having my tonsils removed at age ten	Children who had their tonsils removed have the same upper-respiratory infections in adulthood as those who did not have their tonsils removed.
Being an only child	Most only children, as adults, have more than one child.

After you formulate a hypothesis, you can raise additional questions. The answers to your questions and the way you go about collecting these answers can become the content of your essay, report, or paper.

Here are some of the questions I raised regarding my first hypothesis, "Having a playground created a sense of community among neighborhood residents."

Who used the Prospect Park playground?
What streets did those people live on?
Did mothers use it more than fathers?
What days of the week was it most/least frequented?
When did parents and children stop using the playground?
Did children and/or parents socialize with the other regulars at the playground?
Were the playground regulars different from the park regulars?
Was there an income or education difference between those parents who took their children to the park regularly and those who took them to the playground?

As you can see, my memory of the Prospect Park playground generated questions that could lead to a sociological study of playgrounds as community builders. My hypothesis grew out of my actual experience, not an abstract assignment or intellectual exercise. Most students, however, have not been encouraged to use their own experiences as foundations for research and essays. Instead, most assignments encourage students to borrow generalizations from assignments, clichés, reference books, teachers' essay questions, and essay and research formulas.

You can develop meaningful papers for all of your coursework by allowing your memories to lead the way to your authentic concerns.

Keep a Dialogue Journal for Course Work or Personal Growth

A Dialogue Journal enables you to take charge of your own writing process. It helps you analyze, synthesize, and evaluate your writing. A Dialogue Journal is also valuable when you read, hear a lecture, participate in group discussion, work out a mathematical or scientific problem, study for a test, or work out a personal problem.

Choose a passage, experience, or problem from any of your books or assignments. Describe it in the left-hand column of your notebook and your reaction to or interpretation of it in the right-hand column—as you did with your memories. Ask yourself these questions:

• What strikes me about this piece of writing?
• What are the difficult words or concepts?
• How do I feel about the writing?
• What strategies do I use to solve difficult problems?
• What other writing or experience does this one bring to mind?
• Where can I go for additional information?

Encourage other students to keep the same kind of Dialogue Journal, and then pass your journal around for additional feedback, asking your friends and colleagues to react to your comments. Here is how graduate student Noreen Mallon used a double-entry Dialogue Journal to understand a difficult math problem.

Sample

DIALOGUE JOURNAL: MATH

At first I believed that the solution could be found with an algebraic equation, and I tried to formulate one with two unknowns. I tried adding and multiplying but kept geting nowhere. When I came up with 27 rabbits and 23 chickens I thought I could figure out the answer

Now that I see the algebraic solution, I find that this was a difficult task that I still do not fully understand. "Playing around" with the numbers was too haphazard. A chart provides a more organized approach, but I didn't understand how to begin.

by "playing" (adding here
and taking away there). At
one point I thought I had
the answer—24 rabbits and
22 chickens. However, I
soon realized that this did
not add up to 50 animals.
Again I tried to play around
with the numbers adding
here and taking away there.
By this time, the frustration
was mounting and time was
flying! I returned to the algebraic equations several
times, only to give up in
desperation! I couldn't think
of another way to approach
the problem.

Reread your Dialogue Journal entries before writing a paper or
an exam. Allow yourself to think about the content of the entries.
You do not have to ask more questions. Permit insights and
feelings to come to mind, as they do when you meditate. Record
those insights. For example, "I used to be afraid of math and
used more negative words about it than I do now."

Leave several pages at the end of each area of your Dialogue
Journal so that you can write summaries or conclusions about
your observations. When you summarize or interpret your Dialogue Journal, you will get a good sense of how far you have
come in a subject or relationship and where you would like to
go next.

EXPERIMENT WITH GENRE

When I was a student, I never realized that literary forms could
help me uncover the meaning of an equation or a personal re-

lationship, the results of a scientific experiment or the purpose of a subject, but they can. The typical genres required by schools—lab reports, essays, equations, research papers—can sometimes confine rather than expand your thinking in their disciplines. Use your Dialogue Journal as a crystal to cast a multidimensional light on your learning or on your private life. Before a paper is due, brainstorm ideas by freewriting your assignment in a genre other than the one that is required. For example, write a lab report as a poem, an interpretation of a poem as another poem, an essay as a dialogue, a report as a letter, or an equation as a narrative. You will be surprised at the amount of usable information you can transfer from these exercises to your required papers. You can even investigate various aspects of a personal relationship by using freewriting, dialogues, poetry, or imaginary letters.

Hal Melnick, a math professor at the Bank Street College of Education, asked his math students to write two imaginary letters: One was to a former math teacher, in order to uncover the source of some of their math blocks; the other was to another student, telling him or her about their experiences in his course. He also asked them to keep a daily "Feelings Journal" on their course work. Here are some results of his assignments.

Samples

FEELINGS JOURNAL: GEOMETRY—WHAT IT MAKES ME THINK AND FEEL

So we're doing geometry tomorrow! I get some mixed feelings when I think about it. Part of me remembers Mrs. Loria's tenth-grade class, where we sat and watched her do proofs on the old overhead, day after day after endless boring day.

Somehow, *before* that, I seem to remember that geometry was fun, but I really couldn't remember any specific details. When I'd taught geometry previously, I had been caught in an abyss between relating it to the real world (and making it fun and dynamic!) and using Mrs. Loria's all-important *symbols*.

I can see now that I should have relied less on the symbolic stuff and done more from the concrete. After all, most of the kids weren't "getting" the symbol stuff anyway. I think now that if I got away from the book more, I would do much better and still be following the grade's course of study. Judging by what we have already done in this class, I can't wait to see what's coming next!

MARGIE ROGERS, graduate student, teacher

LETTER TO A FORMER MATHEMATICS TEACHER

Dear Mr. Sharpe,

I'm pretty sure you won't remember me without trying hard, so here are some dates around 1966 and 1967. It was when you taught sixth grade at Pashley to the skip-grade and high-track students. I was one of the girls in your class that year.

I can't remember any student not liking you. We all loved and enjoyed what we did in class. It was not an easy year for me, though. I had trouble understanding some ideas in math right from the first day. Do you remember yelling at me because I didn't understand exponents? I do. I remember crying because I couldn't, and I was so embarrassed I didn't want to frustrate you by being stupid when everyone else understood so easily.

But the idea of exponents just seemed pointless to me the way you explained it. It was like putting a message in code, but not needing anyone to keep it secret from. I needed to know why the code was important, but you never

said why that day. Did you say why that year? I suspect not.
I think you were concentrating on the concept to the ex-
clusion of its applications. I learn by applying. Sometimes
I never understand a concept until I see it *in situ.* I need to
work from the context out each time.

This last month I have been learning how to teach
math a "new" way. I have really been learning how to *learn*
math, though, because I never really made math my own
in the first place. I can see more easily what I really needed
from you and how teaching methods then prevented you
from giving it to me. What a shame. It's easy to see how
in other, more "feminine" subjects, the teaching was different and I did truly comprehend, excel, and earn your
praise. I wish I could have been praised across the board,
however, and I will always regret the feeling of separation
and loss that I had in math during your class.

NOREEN MALLON

LETTER TO A STUDENT

Dear Duke,
I've been going to school to learn how to be a better math
teacher and in the process have become not only a better
teacher but a better person for the experience.

We've spent a lot of time studying about the different
ways that people can learn and about how to help students
become better learners. I can really say that now I understand how you felt after you found out you had a learning
problem—suddenly it all made sense! What an exhilarating
feeling of freedom when all those little pieces fall into place.
For you, it was when you saw that you learn differently from
some people; for me, it was when I saw that I approach
things from a different perspective.

We've spent lots of time working with materials in this

class. Many I'd seen before but never really knew how to use. I still have lots to learn, but I feel like I know how to get started and I'm no longer afraid to try.

Love,
Mrs. Rogers

CONTINUE WITH YOUR WRITING RESPONSE GROUP

A writing response group is important for all writing tasks, not just for memory writing. It is difficult for us to perceive the big and little mistakes we make in our school papers and reports unless we hear about them from our peers. If you continue to write for your teachers' eyes alone, your writing will stay on the level of dull and lifeless school English. The best way to infuse life into your words is by having a real audience respond to your work.

If you are a student, develop a school-assignment writing response group. Your group can help you brainstorm on topics for course papers, focus you on the content and mechanics of your papers, and support your determination to keep your authentic voice. School groups often meet once a month, or they come together before assignment deadlines.

Hang On to Your Writing Voice

You found your writing voice when you wrote about your memories. Don't lose it as you write school-related essays, papers, and reports. Try to remember the way you sounded in your memory writing. Your authentic sound, rhythm, and energy will invigorate your school-related writing if you consciously give yourself permission to make the connection.

Acquiring knowledge is both an inner and an outer journey. We cannot know the world except through the lens of ourselves—

our own biases, experiences, feelings, and memories. Now that you know how to take your childhood memories and shape them into more general statements and hypotheses about the world, you are ready for Chapter 9, which shows what happens to both teachers and their students when teachers write about *their* childhood memories.

9

Teachers as Writers: Sharing Memory Writing

*I've stopped thinking of myself as a performer
and the classroom my stage. Now I think of it as
my home into which forty to fifty students are
invited to spend a year with me and we will get
to know each other and I will learn as much as
or more than they do.*

—DIANE BURKHARDT

When I am filled with an experience, I can't wait to tell others about my discovery. Somehow in the process of telling, I start teaching, and through the teaching process my own learning becomes more rooted and alive.

Those of you who are teachers may already know that there is nothing to be taught to students, there is only that which you create between them, the lesson, and you. Just as writers bring a lifetime of memories to the creation of stories, so teachers bring a different lifetime of experience with which to help students re-create theirs.

Throughout this chapter teachers talk with bubbling enthusiasm about the way writing and sharing childhood memories has transformed their classrooms. These teachers collaborated with their students by sharing their memory writing with them. As a result, both the students' and the teachers' creativity was enhanced: The students become more creative and natural writers, and the teachers became more creative and natural instructors.

READ YOUR WRITTEN MEMORIES TO YOUR YOUNG STUDENTS

> In telling their life stories, people create their own plot lines, establishing the framework in which they live and will live. These life stories reveal what they feel is significant now and in the future.
>
> —JEROME BRUNER

When you bring your childhood into your classroom, you draw on a powerful and fundamental mode of learning—learning through identification. Culture is passed on from adult to young student; youths need to encounter how caring adults have structured their experiences and have developed pathways to the memories that guide their lives.

Read what one teacher, Judy Luster, has to say about this process:

> I start all my writing lessons with my own work now. Not only do students trust me because I share myself with them, but I also get feedback for my own growth as a writer. It's amazing how much I've revised because of what my students have to say. When I read about my memories, I feel that I am letting my students know that I'm human; I make mistakes; I'm just like them; I have good memories and horrible ones, too. They know they can share their real selves because I share mine.
>
> Once after I read a monologue about my fears, one very shy girl in my class talked about how frightened she was. I never dreamed my monologue would be that important to her. She wrote a letter to her sister, and it took her seventeen drafts to get it right. She saw the pride I took in my own writing, and she wanted her letter to be written well.

Encourage your students to struggle to find their voices and to question, contrast, and compare their own experiences with yours. Beneath the surface of our memories are the frameworks we use to view the seemingly unconnected events in our lives. If you leave your memories out of your teaching, you will also leave out the framework of your beliefs, desires, expectations, emotions, and intentions.

Look at what happens when teachers read their memory writing to their students. Says Mary Winsky,

> My students and I are now closer than ever. I read about my childhood to them and I feel I've let them into a part of my life that I never felt teachers were supposed to do— they see me as a person in the process of learning about writing, not just an expert. June did that with us. She modeled so much through her memories that I thought, "If she dared do it with us, I can do it with my kids." They respect me more. I haven't lost my status because I've let them know I'm learning to write along with them.

And for Holly Church,

> I was a teacher trainer, yet when I read my memories to the kids I felt more identified with them than with the teachers. We were all writers together. I even found the writing I had done in undergraduate school and read those pieces too. Before I was encouraged to write about my child-hood I had not thought about sharing *my* writing with my students.

Conversing about your memories with your students not only will build a trusting and empathic classroom but will also become a source of power—power that your students can harness to decode their own realities in relation to yours and the rest of the world's. In so doing, they will establish an autonomy that honors and utilizes the past in their construction of the present and future.

LET YOUR STUDENTS BRING THEIR MEMORIES TO SCHOOL

One must possess one's own picture or "map" of the world before one can
muster much confidence on how to educate, why, or what to educate for.
—MAXINE GREENE *and* MARY ANNE RAYWID

Both Judy Luster and Mary Winsky have become less afraid of
the emotion that comes from authentic writing discourse. Their
own writing response group has rewarded them with the tools
with which to hear and respond to personal material. Their
students know that they can bring their beliefs, desires, expectations, emotions, and intentions to school with them because
their teachers have brought theirs and also because they know
their teachers can help them transform their feelings into writing.

Students who are treated with respect and given a chance
to share their memories can also partake of a whole range of
present personal and emotional material, such as divorce, family
illness, relocation, and school difficulties. The payoff for teachers
who allow their students to bring both their emotional and cog-
nitive selves to school is both an openness to other students and
improved writing from students of varying abilities.

Writes Judy Luster,

A lot of my students had some terrible things happen to
them this year. Several brothers and sisters either died of
cancer or were killed in automobile accidents. One mother
had also died, and another had been diagnosed with cancer.
Because I learned how to give and get responses in our
research group, I could allow my students the freedom to
write about their losses. I knew that I could set up a situation
where they could read what they wrote and I could be assured
that they would get an appropriate uncritical response. I
had them identify with one another by using the exercises,
"when I wrote that" and "imagery feedback."

Some of the most beautiful and well-written pieces came from the students in my class who were supposed to have learning problems. Most of them had never written anything personal before. The feeling in the room when my kids read aloud was so loving and supportive. It was probably one of the high points of my teaching career to have been able to allow that much emotion to come out in my English class.

Some of the students didn't want anyone else but me to read their work. That was OK. They all wanted responses though. I made it clear that they could write and they didn't have to share if they didn't want to. Everyone opted to have someone read and comment on their work. It worries me to think that for years before, students probably were going through the very same traumas but I was too scared to allow that material into my classroom.

Once you invite your students to bring their memories into your classroom, they may tell you things you may not want to know. We are living in a time of transition. Every aspect of our culture as we know it is under siege, and unfortunately our students reflect our culture's turmoil. If we are to help them clarify their thinking and shape the language they will need both to live in and to change our world, we have to listen to who they really are, not who we wish they were. Some of you may be the only one in their lives who will give them time to be themselves. The more you listen to them the more they will be able to listen to you when you converse with them about the way others have lived, loved, and acted in the past. And if you are prepared to listen to the truth of their lives, you in turn will be transformed.

DEVELOP STUDENT-CENTERED WRITING CURRICULA

What empowers . . . is the recognition that there is no "reality" that is unquestionably given, the same for everyone. . . . reality must be understood as interpreted experience, . . . there can be multiple perspectives and multiple interpretations.

—MAXINE GREEN

Groups of teachers all over the country are beginning to weave their writing curricula around their students' experiences. Working collaboratively and sharing the excitement of writing, reading, and learning together, they have substituted packaged, teacherproof material with student-centered, process-writing instruction. Here is how Mary Winsky has integrated her students' interests into the requirements of the curriculum:

I have all these books to teach my students. I used to have them read *The Diary of Anne Frank,* for example, and write a report or essay about it. Now I see that everything I teach can be connected to my students' experiences. I have my students read about Anne Frank, and I've had them write journal entries as if they were Anne. They know how to do this because they keep journals on their own lives. I've also had them write imaginary letters to her, as though she were still alive. I'm using the journals and their literature writing requirements as though they were connected. In my school system no one told me to link them, I just see that they are linked, and I want my students to see that, too. I think that's what teaching is all about.

Teachers like Mary have helped their students learn about the world by integrating their students' beliefs, desires, expectations, emotions, and intentions into the material to be learned.

CREATE A TEACHER RESPONSE GROUP

Good schools are built on the principles of community and the struggle to be human. Unfortunately, many of our schools are dedicated to self-interest and are structured to isolate teachers from healthy decision making and positive social relations.

Teachers flourish when they can talk about their writing and their students' writing in a supportive response group.

Says Jim Wheeler,

> The writing group is my support system. Did you ever hear what teachers talk about in a teachers' room? No one, I mean no one, ever talks about teaching or the really important deep-down things we all carry around with us from day to day. My group is more than a writing group to me; it's my lifeline to what's really important. I need it to center myself. I come to it every Sunday afternoon for three and one-half hours, and I never feel like I'm giving up something. I can't imagine being without it now.

And Holly Church,

> I never knew where my imagery or the group's left off. When we did "imagery feedback" at the end of our sessions and I heard all the images being said and remembered, my own memories were triggered. I think I wrote about Lake Michigan because I heard Mary's lake memory. I can still tell you the collective images one year later. I also became more excited about a good piece of writing—both in the group and in the classroom. My values changed, and I would get ecstatic over a particular line that a child or professional writer wrote.

Teacher response group members photocopy and submit their own or their students' writing to their group. They meet during lunch or free periods, or they arrange to alternate in one another's homes. Some groups alternate between discussing classroom practice and listening to writing.

Underneath the variety of personalities and life-styles is a basic human need to feel loved, listened to, respected, and wanted. Although we are all individuals with different sets of experiences and expectations, we were once all children, too, and that unifies us. With unity comes strength—the strength to make changes in ourselves and in our classrooms and the strength to admit our failures and defeats. Teachers who have learned the value of an interpretive community can transfer their group learning back to their students.

WRITE WITH STUDENTS IN DIALOGUE JOURNALS

When you were keeping a Process Journal, you actually were keeping a Dialogue Journal, in which you held a dialogue between your memory writing and yourself. This is a helpful tool for discovering your writing process, but it can also be used to discover how your students are responding to the writing they are hearing or reading. When your students keep Dialogue Journals, you can give them individual attention even though the limits of your class time may seem to preclude it.

Show your students a copy of one of your notebooks. Explain how it works. Ask them to respond to your memory writing or to one another's writing at least once each week. In turn, you or other students in your class can respond to their comments, and in doing so you all will be engaged in a writing conversation. This conversation translates into potent education.

EMPOWER YOUR STUDENTS AND LEARN TO BE SILENT

English teacher Kathleen Williams tells her students exactly what they will be experiencing during her writing workshop. But then she stands back and keeps *her* creative ideas and solutions out of her students' way. She has learned about the powerful role silence can play in her classroom.

> Mentally I'm tapping my fingers while my students go through the writing process. It empowers students when you let them take ownership of their own writing, but it's so hard for us to let go. We're almost Pavlovian in our response

to kids. The minute we see them quiet or struggling, we want to move right in close and help them, nurture them, put our words in their mouths. But I resist that urge and instead facilitate their learning by saying, "Where are you now?" "Are you stuck?" Or I ask them to tell me—in an instant version—about their writing intentions. I also tell them to watch their digressions because they have a shape all their own. I tell them not to rush the process.

The most difficult part of teaching a process-writing workshop is that I have to take the focus off of me. I am a creative teacher, and I would like to bring all sorts of wonderful ideas to my students. I like to feel responsible for inspiring great writing, but the greatest gift I can give them is themselves. In the long run that is so much better than any formula.

Teachers who bring the writing process and childhood memories into their classrooms recognize that students are born writers just waiting for someone to listen to them with compassion and respect. Much of the art of teaching is embedded in the writing process. The art of living lies just below the surface of our memories as well, and that is the subject of Chapter 10.

10

Come Home: Enhance Your Life Through Childhood Memories

It is then that you will hear a voice within yourself. It was there all the time, but you never listened before . . . it will gradually grow louder and clearer the more you take heed of its message until one day it thunders inside you and you will have come home.

—KRISTIN ZAMBUCKA

We are all people in a hurry, rocketing off toward the future, toward the unknown. Somehow, in the surge forward, memories seem old-fashioned, useless, or backward. But a life that moves forward without a sense of its own personal and social history is fragmented and hollow, lacking a center, soul, and conscience. The childhood memories that had the power to transform you into a writer also have the power to motivate you from within, release your hidden energies and powers, and help you act on your life to transform your reality.

POSITIVE MEMORIES—LEGACY OF PLEASURE

Pleasant memories from childhood help us to celebrate. We collect things; keep diaries; take photographs; write autobiographies, songs, and novels; and daydream to hang on to them. And when our memories of growing up are especially positive, we sometimes want to have children to experience our childhood again through them.

Positive childhood memories can take some of our cares away, no matter where we are—in a hospital, dentist's office, car, classroom, barracks, submarine, or jail. Allow these memories to transform the humdrum parts of your life with refreshing and delightful images and sensations.

NEGATIVE MEMORIES—INSTRUMENTS OF STRENGTH

> The struggle of man against power is the struggle of memory against forgetting.
>
> —MILAN KUNDERA

Although my family, like yours, has many stories to tell, they are not all pleasant. But writing about the overcast—gray, frightening—events of our past can help us take charge of those events, keep track of them over time, and weigh and investigate them so they can be viewed and analyzed in the light of our present maturity and life experience.

A negative memory is like a demon—a demon that can attack and destroy us out of the blue. When we grab hold of it, we can determine whether the toxicity has diminished or increased over time. We can shape the memory so that its claws are trimmed and its jaws are wired shut. If we write about it, we can turn its negative power into inner strength that we can use for the rest of our lives.

Here is what happened when one student, Etta Endahl, allowed herself to write negatively about her mother:

My poems continue to pour out, like blood from a newly cut finger. Working on my memories I touched a deep, secluded place in myself. All those moments, locked so securely all those years, have been tumbling out, screaming to be written. I've had the burden of judging and criticizing my mother as long as I can remember. When I began to write, all that negative stuff had to come out first. It felt like rotten garbage. I didn't feel clean and connected. I felt all squirmy, as if my whole body and being were out of alignment. After it was all out I knew who my mother was. I could accept her gift to me, her feminist spirit, her focus on work, her singlemindedness about her family's education and their place in America.

THE PEOPLE IN YOUR CHILDHOOD: KEY TO YOUR IDENTITY

Memories and reality bear a continuing, reciprocal relationship, influencing and determining one another ceaselessly.

—ERIK ERIKSON

Memorialize your family and friends who are gone. The act of writing in a sense reconstructs them, brings them back to life once more, so that you can benefit from their wisdom and from their mistakes. Elie Wiesel, writer and Holocaust survivor, says, "Remembering, even the negative, when it turns to writing, becomes a 'matzeva,' an invisible tombstone, erected to the memory of the dead unburied. Each word corresponds to a face, a prayer, the one needing the other so as not to sink into oblivion."

Even for those of you whose childhoods were more unpleasant than not, writing about the past can be redemptive. Wiesel continues, "The deeper the nostalgia and the more complete the fear, the richer the word and the secret."

When you write about childhood memories you can bring back the people in your life. In the process of writing you can also discover yourself, as teacher Shelly Duke has done in this piece.

SOMEBODY'S SOMEBODY

I've just come home to my Gormley Avenue apartment after another snowy Toronto funeral. My mother's friend Sophie just died, and I still think of her as "my mother's friend" even though my mother died eight years ago.

It was like that in Kirkland Lake, Ontario, where I grew up. Somehow people died or moved away but remained connected forever. They "belonged" to people because they were someone's friend, someone's father, someone's wife, someone's aunt, someone's nephew. . . . No matter that they might also be a retailer, photographer, teacher, musician, skier, or successful entrepreneur.

As I stood at the grave of my mother's friend Sophie, I found myself staring into the tear-filled eyes of Faye, another one of "my mother's friends." I felt such loss for the solid, strong, and loving Jewish heritage that faces like Faye's had passed on to me in our small community.

It wasn't even that I really knew a lot of those people— not where they came from, what they had lost, or what their dreams were. In fact, I didn't really know my mother's dreams or her heartaches. What I did know was a constant "thereness" in my town—people who were like signposts and places of comfort to me. "Saul's," "The Fashion Centre," "Joe Dash Men's Wear," the movie theaters, "Seymour's," "the Breland's," my grandfather Zayda's place, which became my dad's—"Duke Camera Centre"—all were on the walk I always took as a child, clearly marked by this collection of people who knew how to bury their own dead, cater their own "mitzvahs," play their own music, fight their own battles, and be there for each other.

Whenever I go to a funeral like that of Joe's wife, Sophie, who was Ron's mother and my mother's friend, we all embrace each other and cry, and we say, "It should be on better occasions that we see each other again." But I don't even know a lot of their names anymore or what to say to them except to cry for the ones who are gone now, like my mother and my mother's friend Sophie . . .

But what I have to say to these people never really goes away. And it is, "Thank you for being so rich in spirit and solid and brave and committed and decent and for loving me and watching out for me and being proud of me all these years because I am such an important person. I am Millie and Eddie's daughter, Lorne and Libby's sister; Rick, Leslie, Sandy, Harvey, Belinda, and June's cousin; Sylvia and Don's, Dave and Josie's, Morris and Faye's, Ethel and Lou's niece; Elaine's friend. . . . And I'm also the daughter of the mother who was Sophie's friend. I am somebody's somebody."

Family Memories: Road to Self-Knowledge

Whether or not we like it, we are the beneficiaries of the memories and messages our relatives leave behind for a future they will not see. Their childhood reminiscences can be inspirational and instructive, remnants of our collective heritage. Unfortunately, because many of us are too busy or too frightened to listen to them, our collective legacy has begun to wither and die.

But you will receive a multitude of gifts if you are willing to listen to these memories. Embedded in your family's memories are the hopes, victories, and defeats not only of your loved ones but of the human race. They have "been there" and come back; they have returned from what we will face in the future. Beneath the surface of their stories are the subtle clues that can guide us toward the actions we must take in our lifetime.

Moreover, by listening compassionately, you yourself will be giving a gift to family members who are telling their tales— an opportunity for them to resolve earlier overpowering emotions. Whether family members tell you about their history to resolve painful childhood events or to savor pleasant ones, the telling will release their latent vitality. For the elderly or terminally ill there is an added benefit: This renewed vitality will help them confront and cope with the most important task of their life cycle—preparation for life's end.

Build Family Relationships

Even though we all have different desires, interests, and experiences, we all have one thing in common—our memory of what it felt like to be a child. Look at what happens when families share their recollections. Jim Wheeler writes,

> When I read about my childhood to my children, it helps me to remember what it's like to be a kid. It also helps my son realize that I wasn't so different from the way he is now. It has brought us closer together.

Donna Skolnick says,

> I read all the stories I write to my husband and my children. I reserve Sunday nights. My kids look forward to it. It is a way for them to share in my past and also in my writing process. They get to see that I have a private and creative life. I think it stimulates their creativity too. My daughter and son are keeping journals now. My son, who can't write yet, is keeping a drawing journal about his experiences.

But sometimes sharing is disappointing. Says Holly Church,

> My mother is a writer. She's written children's books. I read her my work. I expected her to say, "Holly, you're terrific; you're a writer!" But instead she said, "Some of this is very good."

Keep on writing. Do not be discouraged or closed-minded if you receive criticism from family members. Listen with two ears—one ear for what your piece is triggering in them and one ear for criticism that may be valid.

Sharing your memories with your family may reconnect them to their ancestors, as it did Judy Luster and her parents.

> I went back to Charles City, and I asked about my grandfather's journal. He wrote about being in the army during

World War I. My aunt had it up in her attic. No one had done anything about copying it, so it had started to turn yellow and fall apart.

I had it copied, and I've got it for safekeeping now. I asked Dad to read it. Mom cried over his poem about war. He wrote lots of day-to-day, routine stuff and about being lonely. My mother didn't know her father had written a word, but I remembered my aunt saying something about it years ago.

Sharing your memories may create a closer bond with your loved ones, or it may point up the need for continued dialogue between various family members. Whatever your family dynamics, your memories may help head your family on the road to becoming more compassionate and sustaining for all its members.

Inform Your Present Life

Memory follows interest. The personal interest of the remember si-
multaneously recalls and transfigures the past.

—WILLIAM JAMES

Patients are considered cured, therapists report, when they can tell their life stories from a revised and compassionate perspective. For example, a neurotic patient may dwell on the devastating effect her father's death had on her relationships with men. But after she has worked through her grief, anger, and fears, her stories about her father may focus more on the strengths she inherited from him than on the hole he left in her life. The facts of her past have not changed—her father is still dead, but her attitude about his death has changed. In turn, that shift in attitude will actually allow her to remember the past differently.

Let me show you how listening to one of my memories transformed my understanding of the past.

ROCK SHOWER: 1945

I was eight, jubilantly throwing rocks one after another across Lincoln Road. I threw so well that many of them skipped up over the curb and onto the sidewalk in front of the corner French cleaners.

My mother's friend, Mrs. Goldberg, who was on her way to Ebinger's bakery, stopped in her tracks as she saw me hurl one mica-encrusted missile after another across the busy one-way street. She grabbed my arm and wiggled her finger in front of my nose. "You're a bad girl," she said. "You could kill someone with those rocks. How would you like it if one of them hit you? I'm going to tell your mother!"

Her admonitions made no sense to me then. Throwing rocks was no one's business but mine, I remember thinking. They weren't hurting anyone. In fact, I was proud that I was timing them so that the projectiles landed when no person or car was coming down the street. It felt absolutely terrific to hurl them in the air and watch them sail clear to the other side of the street, which was to me like a foreign country, for I hadn't yet been given permission to cross it by myself.

I ran home to tell my mother, and she was furious. "You apologize to Mrs. Goldberg the next time you see her," she said. I was filled with dread, shyness, anger, shame. I felt manipulated by my mother, who I thought wanted to get into Mrs. Goldberg's good graces. "I don't want to," I retorted. "It's not her street!" "You have to!" warned my mother, but I didn't feel sorry, and I knew that I would never say it to Mrs. Goldberg, not ever.

"Do you remember when I threw rocks and Mrs. Goldberg caught me?" I recently asked my mother. My mother smiled. "You were such a good girl. You apologized to her that very same day." I had to wonder then: Did I or didn't I apologize? Did I change the story, or did my mother? If I could find Mrs. Goldberg, what story would she tell about that day?

I needed to remember throwing rocks as a sign of independence, bravery, and self-assertion. But my mother needed to focus on my obedience, which helped her feel like a successful parent. The "rock shower" incident means one thing to me and another to my mother, because we select and interpret our memories according to who we are at any given moment. For this reason your memories are valuable maps that can lead you to the treasure of your present unconscious and conscious goals, concerns, dreams, and desires.

LIBERATE YOURSELF—FICTIONALIZE YOUR CHILDHOOD

To write good fiction you need complete visual recall of what didn't happen.

—MARY LEE SETTLE

Much of my childhood was spent doing what other people wanted me to do—eating all the food on my plate, not talking back, saying please and thank you, being careful, being awfully "good" all the time! Just once in my life, I wanted to describe a childhood event in which I rebelled, was in charge, could control others. But I had none, so I made some up instead. It was absolutely liberating. To my amazement and delight *my fictionalized memory had the same effect on my present life as if it had actually happened.* That is, it made me feel good to imagine an event where I finally won out over my oppressors—parents, teachers, and bossy kids.

For instance, for the past few years I have been wondering what I would have been like if I had gone to some of the forbidden places in my childhood—like the roof of our building, the park at night, the basement where coal was delivered, the courtyard behind our house. All seemed so fascinating and mysterious. Would I be a different person today if I had broken those rules then?

Here is a poem I wrote about an adventure I had with my cousin Harvey. I will tell you—after you read it—what actually happened, what I made up, and why.

LIES?

"Let's ride the elevator,
I'll push the buttons,"
my cousin Harvey said.
"I'll get you to the roof
without even stretching."

When we rode together
I wasn't afraid we'd
get stuck between floors,
or that my father would
catch me riding for fun.
"Hold my hand," he said.
"I'll show you how tiny
everything looks from
way 'up high."

"The next time we're in the park,
I'll catch you a catfish
with my bare hands," Harvey
pledged as we strolled closer to
the edge of the roof.
"You're so pretty,
I'm going to marry you
when I grow up."

The wet clothes on the line
flapped at our backs as we
gazed past Flatbush Avenue
to the rowboats floating
on the dark green lake
nestled in the heart of
the Park.

"If this black tar didn't
stick to our shoes we could fly

together over the clotheslines
clear to the Brooklyn Bridge,"
Harvey crooned, and I nodded,
yes, oh yes.

We rode down to dinner,
flushed with plans.
"Where have you two been?" the
grown-ups nagged. "Out front
playing Red Light, Green Light
and Ring-a-Levio," I lied
with my fingers crossed.

Later, in my teens I ran around
with forbidden boys,
danced at Roseland,
and cut French to ride the
subway into Manhattan
with Sybil and her
boyfriend, Fred.

And lately, I've been
writing poems that show me
crossing streets against
the light, skating on
thin ice, or necking
in the dark alley behind our
house; but those weren't
the worst lies I've told.

This one was:
When my cousin Harvey got married,
moved to Manhattan, and changed
his name to Darius,

I said I didn't care.

I never went on the roof with my cousin Harvey. I did run around with boys my parents did not like, and I did cut class and hang around with my friends Sybil and Fred. Furthermore, Harvey and I did talk about getting married when we grew up, even though we were cousins and it was taboo. He did move away—in fact, so far away that to this day no one in our family knows where he is. Before he moved he told me that he had changed his name from Harvey to Darius. I didn't know, until I wrote about myself up on the roof, that I had been hurt when he left me for his own life. I also did not know that I was looking for some early clues to his later disappearance. I might never have discovered the depth of my feelings for him had I not imagined us at the edge of the roof together.

CALL YOURSELF TO ACTION

Writing about your childhood can change your attitude toward your present relationships. Writing helps you to uncover your real feelings, interests, and concerns so that not only can you reflect upon them but you can also do something about them. That doing may range from a subtle shift in consciousness to an actual change in the style and manner in which you conduct your life. Mary Winsky says,

My mother had me when she was thirty-six. I saw her as a contemporary when I was writing about her. I could understand her and myself better. She wanted to keep me so safe as a teenager. I had curfews; she forgot laughter. I admire her for taking care of my grandmother before she died, and not letting me notice she was doing it. My clothes were washed and ironed. My mother may not know outwardly that I forgive her but I do; I love her more now.

And Heidi Steinberg, another student, reveals how writing about her family changed her attitude and her actions toward her mother and others:

> Confidential mother-daughter chats are rare. I am free, but something is missing. The silence, now that it is permissible, is not comfortable.
>
> So, I break it. I start small by inviting them to my house. We talk about my work with children and their retirement.
>
> "Everyone says we should look for volunteer work, try Florida, travel," Mom says, sipping wine.
>
> "Enjoy your free time, Mom. Enjoy Daddy. You're allowed to have unstructured time. Celebrate."
>
> I nuzzle in her arms before they leave. Her full bosom is comforting, warm. She looks teary.
>
> "I hate to say good-bye," she whispers.
>
> Stroking her back, I answer, "Call me when you get home." Every door must be open.
>
> I feel the movement of live language between us carrying fragile emotions.
>
> I think we are making progress. I try on the old ways of women needing women. They are like old clothes one finds in the attic. I am reminded of William Finch in the Bradbury story "A Scent of Sarsaparilla." He went into the attic, fell in love with the past, and never returned. Am I romanticizing the past, overlooking its faults?
>
> I take the risk anyway. Why? There must be hope and joy in my life. Dialogue is a woman's legacy. Why? Life is linear; no one moment can be relived, so all moments are precious. Ritual frames these moments. Rituals are precious again. I am in love. Marriage is possible. Perhaps family. Perhaps a daughter of my own.

NOT AN ENDING

Though I may travel far I will meet only what I carry with me.
—KRISTIN ZAMBUCKA

I hope that you will not lose your childhood sensibility. It can be a fount and a source for your growth as a writer and person. You have learned, hand in hand with me, how childhood memories can lead you to any topic at all—your children, yourself, your dreams, your work, your studies, your relationships, the world—as it might be in the future or was in the past. Whatever you choose to write about after you close this book, may you enjoy the journey itself as much as the destination you seek.

Bibliography

Writers on Writing

Baldwin, Christina. *One to One: Self-Understanding Through Journal Writing.* New York: M. Evans & Company, 1977.

Brande, Dorothea. *Becoming a Writer.* Los Angeles: Jeremy P. Tarcher, 1981.

Elbow, Peter. *Writing with Power.* New York: Oxford University Press, 1981.

Gardner, John. *On Becoming a Novelist.* New York: Harper & Row, 1983.

Melhem, D. H. *Reaching Exercises: The IWWG* [International Women's Writing Guild] *Workshop Book.* New York: Dovetail Press, 1981.

Progoff, Ira. *At a Journal Workshop.* New York: Dialogue House, 1975.

Rainer, Tristine. *The New Diary.* Los Angeles: Jeremy P. Tarcher, 1978.

Winokur, Jon, ed. *Writers on Writing.* Philadelphia: Running Press, 1986.

Zinsser, William. *On Writing Well.* New York: Harper & Row, 1980.

———.*Writing with a Word Processor.* New York: Harper & Row, Colophon Books, 1983.

Teaching Writing

Calkins, Lucy. *The Art of Teaching Writing.* Portsmouth, N.H.: Heinemann Educational Books, 1986.

———. *Lessons from a Child.* Portsmouth, N.H.: Heinemann Educational Books, 1983.

Camp, Gerald, ed. *Teaching Writing: Essays from the Bay Area Writing Project.* Upper Montclair, N.J.: Boynton/Cook Publishers, 1982.

Emig, Janet. *The Web of Meaning: Essays on Writing, Teaching, Learning, and Thinking.* Upper Montclair, N.J.: Boynton/Cook Publishers, 1983.

Fulwiler, Toby, ed. *The Journal Book.* Portsmouth, N.H.: Boynton/Cook Publishers, 1987.

Fulwiler, Toby, and Art Young, eds. *Writing Across the Disciplines.* Portsmouth, N.H.: Boynton/Cook Publishers, 1986.

Gere, Anne Ruggles, ed. *Roots in the Sawdust: Writing to Learn Across the Disciplines.* Urbana, Ill.: National Council of Teachers of English, 1985.

Graves, Donald. *Writing: Teachers and Children at Work.* Portsmouth, N.H.: Heinemann Educational Books, 1983.

Graves, Donald, and Virginia Stuart. *Write from the Start: Tapping Your Child's Natural Writing Ability.* New York: E. P. Dutton, 1985.

Macrorie, Ken. *Telling Writing*. Rochelle Park, N.J.: Hayden Book Company, 1970.

Moffett, James. *Active Voice: A Writing Program Across the Curriculum*. Upper Montclair, N.J.: Boynton/Cook Publishers, 1981.

————. *Coming on Center: English Education in Evolution*. Upper Montclair, N.J.: Boynton/Cook Publishers, 1981.

Murray, Donald. *A Writer Teaches Writing*. Boston: Houghton Mifflin Company, 1968.

————. *Write to Learn*. New York: Holt, Rinehart & Winston, 1984.

Perl, Sondra, and Nancy Wilson. *Through Teachers' Eyes: Portraits of Writing Teachers at Work*. Portsmouth, N.H.: Heinemann Educational Books, 1986.

Rico, Gabriele Lusser. *Writing the Natural Way*. Los Angeles: Jeremy P. Tarcher, 1984.

Schiflett, Betty. "Story Workshop as a Method of Teaching Writing." *College English* 35, no. 2 (1973): 141–60.

Weber, Bruce. *Look Who's Talking*. New York: Pocket Books, Washington Square Press, 1987.

Meditation

Dass, Ram. *Journey of Awakening: A Meditator's Guidebook*. New York: Bantam Books, 1981.

Goleman, Daniel. *Varieties of the Meditative Experience*. New York: E. P. Dutton, 1977.

Hendricks, Gay, and Thomas Roberts, *The Second Centering Book: More Awareness Activities for Children, Parents, and Teachers*. Englewood Cliffs, N.J.: Prentice-Hall, 1977.

Herrigel, Eugene. *Zen and the Art of Archery*. New York: Random House, 1974.

Levine, Stephen. *A Gradual Awakening*. New York: Doubleday, Anchor Press, 1978.

McDonald, Kathleen. *How to Meditate*. London: A Wisdom Basic Book, 1984.

Periodicals

Berthoff, Ann E., ed. *Correspondences*. Boynton/Cook Publishers, P.O. Box 860, Upper Montclair, N.J. 07043.

Dillon, David, ed. *Language Arts: Official Journal of the National Council of Teachers of English*. 1111 Kenyon Road, Urbana, Ill. 61801.

Fearing, Bertie E., and John C. Hutchens, eds. *Teaching English in the Two-Year College*. Urbana, Ill.: National Council of Teachers of English.

Gray, Donald, ed. *College English*. Urbana, Ill.: National Council of Teachers of English.

Nilsen, Alleen Pace, and Ken Konelson, eds. *English Journal*. Urbana, Ill.: National Council of Teachers of English.

Memory-Related Books

Baker, Russell. *Growing Up.* New York: Congdon & Weed, 1982.

Baldwin, James. *Notes of a Native Son.* Boston: Beacon Press, 1968.

Bateson, Mary Catherine. *With a Daughter's Eye.* New York: William Morrow, 1984.

Bly, Robert. *The Man in the Black Coat Turns.* New York: Dial Press, 1981.

Bruner, Jerome. *Actual Minds, Possible Worlds.* Cambridge, Mass.: Harvard University Press, 1986.

———. *On Knowing: Essays for the Left Hand.* Cambridge, Mass.: Harvard University Press, 1982.

Cabral, Olga. *Occupied Country.* New York: New Rivers Press, 1976.

Campbell, Joseph. *Myths to Live By.* New York: Bantam Books, 1975.

Capote, Truman. *Answered Prayers.* New York: Random House, 1987.

Cassirer, Ernst. *An Essay on Man: An Introduction to a Philosophy of Human Culture.* New Haven: Yale University Press, 1944.

Charlton, James, ed. *The Writer's Quotation Book: A Literary Companion.* New York: Pushcart Press, 1980.

Conroy, Pat. *The Prince of Tides.* Boston: Houghton Mifflin Company, 1986.

Curry, Peggy Simson. *Creating Fiction from Experience.* Boston: The Writer, 1964.

DeLillo, Don. *White Noise.* New York: The Viking Press, 1985.

Dillard, Annie. *Teaching a Stone to Talk: Expeditions and Encounters.* New York: Harper & Row, 1982.

Eliot, T. S. *Four Quartets.* New York: Harcourt Brace Jovanovich, 1943.

Erikson, Erik. *Identity and the Life Cycle.* New York: The Macmillan Company, 1957.

Fell, Mary. *The Persistence of Memory.* New York: Random House, 1984.

Greene, Maxine, and Mary Anne Raywid. "Changing Perspectives on Schools." In *Society as Education in an Age of Transition: Eighty-sixth Yearbook of the National Society for the Study of Education.* Edited by Kenneth Benne and Steven Tozer. Chicago: University of Chicago Press, 1987.

Ginsberg, Allen. *Kaddish and Other Poems, Nineteen Fifty-eight to Nineteen Sixty.* San Francisco: City Lights, 1961.

Hahn, Hannelore. *On the Way to Feed the Swans.* New York: Tenth House Enterprises, 1982.

Hall, Donald. *String Too Short to Be Saved: Recollections of Summers on a New England Farm.* Boston: David R. Godine, Nonpareil Books, 1983.

Houston, Jean. *The Possible Human.* Los Angeles: Jeremy P. Tarcher, 1982.

James, William. *The Principles of Psychology,* vol. 1. London: Constable Press, 1950.

Janeczko, Paul B., ed. *Strings: A Gathering of Family Poems.* New York: The Macmillan Company, 1984.

John-Steiner, Vera. *Notebooks of the Mind: Explorations of Thinking*. Albuquerque: University of New Mexico Press, 1985.

Jong, Erica. *Half-Lives*. New York: Holt, Rinehart & Winston, 1973.

Jung, Carl. *Memories, Dreams, Reflections*. Translated by Aniela Jaffé. New York: Pantheon Books, 1963.

Kaminsky, Marc, and Leon Supraner. *Daily Bread*. Urbana: University of Illinois Press, 1982.

Keen, Sam. *To a Dancing God*. New York: Harper & Row, 1970.

Kundera, Milan. *The Book of Laughter and Forgetting*. New York: Alfred A. Knopf, 1980.

Lifshin, Lyn, ed. *Tangled Vines: A Collection of Mother and Daughter Poems*. Boston: Beacon Press, 1978.

Loftus, Elizabeth. *Memory: Surprising New Insights into How We Remember and Why We Forget*. Reading, Mass.: Addison-Wesley, 1980.

McConkey, James. *Court of Memory*. New York: E. P. Dutton, 1983.

Maxwell, William. *Ancestors: A Family History*. New York: Alfred A. Knopf, 1971.

Melhem, D. H. *Rest in Love*. New York: Dovetail Press, 1978.

Merleau-Ponty, Maurice. *The Phenomenology of Perception*. Translated by Colin Smith. London: Routledge & Kegan Paul, 1962.

Montaigne, Michel de. *The Complete Works of Montaigne*. Translated by Donald Frame. Stanford, Calif.: Stanford University Press, 1957.

Morrison, Toni. *Beloved*. New York: Alfred A. Knopf, 1987.

Myerhoff, Barbara. *Number Our Days*. New York: E. P. Dutton, 1978.

Nabokov, Vladimir. *Speak, Memory*. New York: G. P. Putnam's Sons, 1966.

Neisser, Ulric, ed. *Memory Observed: Remembering in Natural Contexts*. San Francisco: W. H. Freeman & Company, 1982.

Nin, Anaïs. *A Woman Speaks: The Lectures, Seminars, and Interviews of Anaïs Nin*. Chicago: Swallow Press, 1975.

Oberski, Jona. *Childhood*. Translated by Ralph Manheim. New York: Doubleday, 1983.

Olney, James, ed. *Autobiography: Essays Theoretical and Critical*. Princeton: Princeton University Press, 1980.

————. *Metaphors of Self: The Meaning of Autobiography*. Princeton: Princeton University Press, 1980.

Olsen, Tillie, ed. *Mother to Daughter—Daughter to Mother: A Feminist Press Daybook and Reader*. Old Westbury, N.Y.: Feminist Press, 1984.

Payne, Karen, ed. *Between Ourselves: Letters Between Mothers and Daughters*. Boston: Houghton Mifflin Company, 1983.

Piercy, Marge. *My Mother's Body*. New York: Alfred A. Knopf, 1985.

Proust, Marcel. *Remembrance of Things Past*. Translated by C. K. Scott Moncrieff, Terence Kilmartin, and Andreas Mayor. New York: Vintage Books, 1982.

Richards, Mary Caroline. *The Crossing Point: Selected Talks and Writings.* Middletown, Conn.: Wesleyan University Press, 1973.

Rodriguez, Richard. *Hunger of Memory.* New York: Bantam Books, 1983.

Rosenblatt, Louise. *Literature as Exploration.* New York: Barnes & Noble, 1976.

Rukeyser, Muriel. *The Collected Poems of Muriel Rukeyser.* New York: McGraw-Hill, 1978.

Sarton, Mary. *Writings on Writing.* Orono, Me.: Puckerbrush Press, 1980.

Sarton, May. *Collected Poems: 1930–1973.* New York: W. W. Norton, 1974.

————. *Journal of a Solitude.* New York: W.W. Norton, 1973.

Sartre, Jean-Paul. *The Words.* Translated by Irene Clephmer. Harmondsworth: Penguin Books, 1964.

Sarraute, Nathalie. *Childhood.* Translated by Barbara Wright. New York: George Braziller, 1983.

Scott-Maxwell, Florida. *The Measure of My Days.* New York: Alfred A. Knopf, 1968.

Simon, Kate. *Bronx Primitive.* New York: The Viking Press, 1983.

Stephens, James. *The Crock of Gold.* New York: The Macmillan Company, 1960.

Strand, Mark. *Selected Poems.* New York: Atheneum Publishers, 1980.

Thoreau, Henry David. *Walden, and Civil Disobedience, Life in the Woods.* New York: W.W. Norton, 1966.

Walker, Alice. "Women." In *Revolutionary Petunias and Other Poems.* New York: Harcourt Brace Jovanovich, 1971.

Welty, Eudora. *One Writer's Beginnings.* Cambridge, Mass.: Harvard University Press, 1984.

Wheelwright, Philip. *The Burning Fountain: A Study in the Language of Symbolism.* Bloomington: Indiana University Press, 1968.

Whitman, Ruth. *Tamsen Donner: A Woman's Journey.* Cambridge, Mass.: Alicejamesbooks, 1977.

Wright, Richard. *Black Boy.* New York: Harper & Brothers, 1945.

Zambucka, Kristin. *Ano' Ano: The Seed.* Honolulu: Mana Publishing Company, 1984.

Reference Books

Fredette, Jean M. *The Fiction Writer's Market.* Cincinnati: Writer's Digest Books. Published annually.

Fulton, Len, ed. *The International Directory of Little Magazines and Small Presses.* Paradise, Calif.: Dustbooks. Published annually.

Judson, Jerome, and Katherine Jobst, eds. *Poet's Market.* Cincinnati: Writer's Digest Books. Published annually.